Contents

Acknowledgments

The Culinary Institute of America wishes to recognize the contribution of the following individuals for their work on this book:

Ben Fink and Dennis Gottlieb for the beautiful photography.

We are grateful to the many individuals who modeled their hands in the photographs: Mark Ainsworth, Olivier Andreini, C.M.C, Ryan Baxter, John DeShetler, David Kamen, Anthony Ligouri, Frank Lopez, and Hinnerk von Bargen.

The countless craftsmen who with each new generation made tools combining skill and artistry.

We also wish to thank chefs Robert Briggs and Gregory Fatigati for their expert reviews of the manuscript and their consultation on the photography.

Finally, a big thank you to Warren Kitchen & Cutlery in Rhinebeck, New York. Richard Von Husen and James Zitz, co-owners of the store, graciously provided many of the tools featured in the book.

Preface

The tools we use in the kitchen today are remarkably similar to those developed thousands of years ago. Technical advances and research in the construction of knives and other basic culinary tools have led to refinements in metal alloys, the ability to refine an edge to a specific task, and adjustments to the shape and construction of a blade to prevent fatigue and stress. During all these years, however, the basics of a good tool's shape and function and the skills necessary to use tools properly have remained constant.

The chef's knife, though not the only tool a chef must master, is generally the knife a novice first learns to use, as well as the one a professional picks up most often. This knife is the most versatile tool in any kitchen because of the many ways in which a skilled hand can work it. In order to develop this accomplished hand, it is important to study, analyze, and practice many cutting techniques used in handling your chef's knife. From this good foundation, it is a simple matter to move on to more specialized knives, including slicers and boning and filleting knives. These can all be mastered easily through practice. As you work with your knives, you will develop a rhythm, learn to coordinate hand motions with cutting tasks, and develop a sense of confidence.

A culinarian must respect knives. Respect grows out of an understanding of the knife's qualities—its proper use, its feel in your hand, and its inherent dangers. *In the Hands of a Chef* addresses all that you must know to develop the confidence and expertise necessary to relax into your work. Relaxation is not the same thing as laziness or lack of attention. It is the feeling of working *with* the tool rather than against it.

The novice cook will find information about, and skills and procedures for, using knives properly and safely in the kitchen. Chefs charged with training their staff will find this a useful, thorough training tool, progressing from basic knife-handling skills, such as steeling and sharpening, to more complex meat fabrication and carving techniques.

A knife that fits your hand and is in prime cutting condition feels like a natural part of your hand. When your skills are as practiced and habitual an activity as driving a car or dialing a phone, you are well on your way to mastery. Here's to your success!

Introduction

Say the word *chef* and you can almost hear the ringing of knives as they flash back and forth on a steel, the rhythmic knocking of a knife chopping, and the whisper of mincing. You can see the gleam of a blade as it flies through an onion. Knives are so much a part of the chef's work that it is impossible to imagine a chef at work without them. As a result, chefs have a strong and personal attachment to their knives.

Today's cooks and chefs have a wide array of cutting tools available to them. A basic selection of tools, the chef's knife kit, is indispensable. Knives (including chef's knives, utility and paring knives, boning and filleting knives, and specialty knives) are part of this selection, along with the appropriate sharpening tools (steels and stones). Other tools, such as peelers, zesters, brushes, palette knives, oyster and clam knives, and metal and wooden spoons, are also so fundamental to kitchen work that they are considered basics.

When you become a good cook, you become a good craftsman first. You repeat and repeat and repeat until your hands know how to move without thinking about it.

— Jacques Pépin

KNIVES AND CUTTING TOOLS

1

The importance of knives to a professional chef or cook cannot be overstated.

High-quality, well-made, well-maintained knives are fundamental kitchen tools that form the foundation of a professional's work.

The "perfect" knife depends upon a variety of factors. The knife should fit your hand, feel substantial but not heavy, and should be well balanced. In the last decade or so, traditional Western-style knives, long the standard of highest quality in knives, have been joined by a number of Eastern-style knives. Both knife-making traditions have resulted in a wide array of knives, some of which can be used for a variety of cutting tasks and some crafted to perform one specific function.

A true professional could get good—even great—results from a lesser-quality knife, but it is harder work. Those same tools in the hands of a novice might make work discouragingly difficult, even impossible. The best tools make it easier for the beginner to learn cutting skills properly, right from the start. It is well worth spending the time and money necessary to get a good knife and become comfortable with the skills involved in sharpening, steeling, and using knives for a variety of cutting tasks.

The chef's knife, as the most basic, all-purpose knife, shares similarities with many other knives, from paring knives to boning knives, scimitars to slicers. Even cleavers are made up of the same basic parts. The following discussion of the parts of a knife uses a chef's knife as the model of the typical knife, made up of a blade and a handle. Knowing how each of these parts can be manufactured and shaped will help you to select any knife with care.

A Brief History of Cutting Tools

Stone cutting tools unearthed by the famed archeologist Richard Leaky at the Koobi Fora site in Kenya are believed to be nearly 3 million years old. They are considered the oldest known man-made tools. Before humans learned to mine and smelt metals, knives had to be produced from found materials, primarily flint and obsidian. Flint, a stone particularly suited to taking an edge, was worked to create a thin cutting edge. Obsidian, a volcanic glass, took a better edge, held it longer, and was more durable than flint, but it was not as widely available. Although obsidian flakes are exceptionally sharp and durable, neither flint nor obsidian is a perfect knife material.

As time went by and the skills necessary to extract pure metals from the mineral deposits above and below the earth were perfected, new materials more suitable for knife blades and other cutting tools were discovered. By about 6500 B.C.E., the skills of mining and extracting soft metals such as copper, lead, and gold from ore had become more widely practiced. These metals were easy to extract from the ore in which they were found and were also soft enough to work while cold. However, these pure metals were too soft to make durable knives for cooking and hunting.

When pure metals are blended with other metals or minerals, metal alloys are created that have their own distinct properties. By about 3500 B.C.E., copper was being alloyed with tin to form the harder, more utilitarian bronze in some parts of southeastern Asia. The practice spread to Europe by about 1800 B.C.E.

Iron, which on its own is quite brittle, prone to rusting, and very hard, can be blended with other materials to make the metal soft enough to take an edge, flexible enough to prevent it from shattering and breaking, and less likely to pit, rust, or discolor. Iron smelting, the first step in producing steel, began around 2000 B.C.E., although tools made from steel were not widely available at first because early steel-making processes were difficult and dangerous.

Early versions of steel show some of the refinements possible when iron is blended with carbon. Originally, the carbon was the ash residue left in the forge after burning the coal or wood to heat the forge. Over time, as metalsmiths learned to control the amount of carbon they added to the iron, a metal known as carbon steel was developed. Low-carbon steel (resembling modern-day wrought iron) was first developed in the Middle East circa 1000 B.C.E., but it was not until 700 B.C.E. that steel tools became common throughout Europe, Asia, and North Africa. Made mostly in small forges and for the purpose of weaponry, the design and production of knives stayed much the same until cutlery for the purpose of dining began to appear in the homes of the nobility. By the sixteenth century C.E., knives, as well as spoons and forks, were established parts of European culture.

Although there was still a great deal more to learn about creating a metal that was durable, flexible, and able to take and hold a sharp edge, these preliminary advances in metal manufacture and the production of tools and knives paved the way for the development of cutting tools similar in nearly all respects to the fine tools used by professional chefs and home cooks today.

Gradual improvements in furnaces allowed metalsmiths to better control the amount of the carbon added to steel. Near the end of the nineteenth century C.E., several rapid advances in steel manufacturing led to the large-scale production of carbon steel of consistent quality. As carbon steel became widely available and affordable, knives made from this material became the norm. This remained the case until the early 1900s, since carbon steel's specific advantages make it well suited to kitchen work. It is durable and hard enough to take an edge but soft enough to allow for reshaping the edge with steels or sharpening stones. If the metal is carefully tempered, it can be made flexible enough for most kitchen work.

Despite all its clear advantages over other materials used to make kitchen knives, there are still some disadvantages to carbon steel. Although it takes a good edge with little effort, the edge deteriorates relatively quickly. This means carbon knives require more upkeep. Carbon steel also rusts, pits, and becomes stained in contact with water and high-acid foods. These knives require careful cleaning and drying before storage, even for a short period.

In 1912, it was discovered that adding chromium to carbon steel inhibits rusting and staining. This metal is called stainless steel. However, stainless steel is harder than carbon steel, making it more difficult for kitchen workers to keep the blade's edge in good shape. Although some specialty knives and many surgical instruments are still made from stainless steel, it wasn't until the development of high-carbon stainless steel around 1920 that carbon steel was replaced as the metal of choice for kitchen blades.

High-carbon stainless steel is produced by blending iron, carbon, chromium, and other metals, such as molybdenum, in a specific ratio to form a blade that is stainless, resilient, and capable of receiving and holding a sharp edge. Although other blade materials, such as stainless-steel alloys (the so-called super stainless steel) and ceramic blades, have since been discovered, high-carbon stainless steel is still used to make the majority of professional-quality knives today.

Damascus Steel

Damascus steel, which has streaks and ripples of carbon across the face of the blade, is becoming popular in both Western and Eastern knives. Named for Damascus, the capital of Syria, and popularized by the Islamic armies of the second crusade (twelfth century C.E.), the technique was originally developed and perfected in India, where the metal was called *wootz*. The steel has an extremely high carbon content (nearing 2 percent carbon). Steel, iron, and carbon are placed within a ceramic container known as a crucible, and then exposed to extremely high heat. The excess carbon bonds with other substances in the metals and precipitates to the surface, where it creates the metal's unique rippled pattern. Today's Damascus steel blades may be made by a different, modern method in which soft- and hard-carbon steels are folded together, then treated with acid. The acid eats through the metals at different rates, creating similar streaks.

The Parts of a Knife

A knife is constructed from several parts, each of which plays a role in the utility, balance, and longevity of the whole. Newer materials have replaced some traditional ones; bone handles are not ordinarily found on kitchen knives today, for example, but composition materials are increasingly common. This section describes the function of each part of the knife and how the parts are put together to form a high-quality tool.

The Blade

Metal knife blades are either forged or stamped.

Forged blades are made by heating a rod (also referred to as a bar or ingot) of high-carbon stainless steel to around 1700°F. The heated metal is set on a handle and then struck with a hammer to pound it to the correct shape and thickness. One

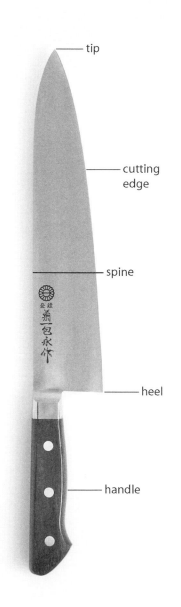

tip

cutting edge

spine

heel

handle

Anatomy of a chef's knife.

of the advantages of a forged blade is that its thickness tapers from the spine to the edge and from the heel to the tip, which gives it the correct balance. After the blade is shaped, it is tempered by heating the blade and then cooling it to improve its strength and durability. Forged blades are generally more durable, better balanced, and of good quality. They tend to be more expensive than stamped blades, however.

Stamped blades are made by rolling the steel into sheets and then cutting out blade-shaped pieces. These blades are of a uniform thickness and may be lighter than some forged blades. Today's stamped blade knives are better balanced than their predecessors, and improved techniques for tempering the metal has also improved their durability and quality.

Japanese sword makers developed techniques to forge and temper the metal distinctly different from those used by Western smiths. First, steel is beaten into sheets and folded repeatedly, and, finally, the metal is slowly tempered in warm water. This refolding and slow tempering make the steel stronger and harder than Western forms of carbon steel.

After the blade is shaped by either forging or stamping, the edge is created. Several types of edges can be used to create a knife, depending upon the intended use.

Taper-Ground Edge The sides of the blade taper smoothly from the blade's thickest point, at the spine, to a narrow V-shaped edge. The angle of the V can be gentle or extremely severe, almost wedge-like. Taper-ground blades are well suited to general-purpose knives and those used for heavy cutting and chopping work since they keep the blade quite stable.

Hollow-Ground Edge The sides of the blade near the edge are ground away to form a hollow, giving the blade an extremely sharp edge. The greater the arc of the hollow, the sharper the edge. Hollow-ground blades are well suited to carving and slicing tasks.

Serrated or Sawtooth Edge The edge is shaped into a row of teeth that can be set very closely or more widely apart. Teeth that can bite make this a good edge for slicing foods with a crust or a firm skin, such as bread, tomatoes, and melons.

Scalloped Edge The edge is ground into a series of small arcs, making it easier to grip and cut into foods. Scalloped blades are used for slicing many of the same foods as serrated blades.

Granton Edge This edge is made by grinding ovals into the sides of the blade, alternating the position on either side of the blade. This makes it less likely that moist cooked meats and fish, especially smoked salmon or gravlax, will stick to the blade.

Single-Sided Edge This style of blade is found most often in Eastern-style knives. Rather than both sides being ground down, only one side is ground, creating a wedge-shaped cutting edge. The angle created by the single edge is more extreme, which means that while the knife is sharper, its edge is more fragile.

The Bolster

In some knives there is a collar or shank, known as a bolster, at the point where the blade meets the handle. The bolster gives the blade greater stability and strength, making it easier and safer to chop through bones, shells, and other hard objects. Some chefs prefer knives with bolsters and consider them to be a sign of a well-made knife that will hold up for a long time. Some knives may have a collar that looks like a bolster but is actually a separate piece attached to the handle. These knives tend to come apart easily and should be avoided. Asian-style knives do not typically have a bolster; however, this is not necessarily a sign of poor craftsmanship.

The Tang

The tang is actually a part of the blade itself. It is the point at which the handle is attached to the knife. Tangs may be full, partial, or rat-tail.

Full Tang A full tang extends the entire length of the handle, giving the knife a greater heft in the handle. Knives with a full tang are sturdy, well balanced, and long-lasting. Full tangs are essential for heavy work; chef's knives or cleavers should have a full tang.

Partial Tang A partial tang does not run the full length of the handle. Although blades with partial tangs are not as durable as those with full tangs, they are acceptable for less frequently used knives or those used for lighter work, such as bread knives, paring or utility knives, and some slicers.

Rat-Tail Tang Rat-tail tangs are much thinner than the spine of the blade and are encased in the handle, which means that they are not visible at the top or bottom edges. The tang is heated and then inserted into the handle. As it burns its way into the handle material, it creates a strong, secure bond between the knife and the handle. Rat-tail tangs were once considered a sign of an inferior knife that would not hold up to heavy use; it is true that this style of knife manufacture was less expensive and was once a sign of a cheaper knife. However, this is not automatically true in all cases. In fact, certain high-quality Japanese-style knives with wooden handles often feature a rat-tail tang.

The Handle

Knife handles are made of various materials, including hard woods with very tight grain, such as walnut or rosewood (often impregnated with plastic), as well as textured metal, and composition materials (vinyl). Some are cushioned to make long hours of work less fatiguing.

Wooden handles are attached to the blade with rivets. If rivets are visible on the handle (they are not always), they should lie flush with the surface of the handle to prevent irritation to the hand and to avoid creating pockets where microorganisms could gather. Composition handles are molded onto the tang.

You will hold your knife for extended periods, so be sure the material and the shape of the handle feel comfortable in your hand. Many manufacturers produce several lines of knives so they can offer a range of handle sizes. People with very small or very large hands should be sure that they are not straining their grip to hold the handle. Western-style knife handles are normally meant for use by either right- or left-handed individuals. The handles on Eastern-style knives are more likely to be produced with specific handedness in mind.

LEFT TO RIGHT Serrated slicer, *sujihiki* (slicer), two utility knives (the first one with granton edge), paring knife, two chef's knives, *yo-deba*, *gyuto*.

Types of Knives

As you learn to work in a professional kitchen, you will want to have the correct tools for certain tasks, but that does not mean that you need to acquire every knife under the sun in order to do most kitchen tasks efficiently. You should decide to purchase a special knife only after evaluating whether your work requires it.

The list that follows is intended as a guide to the knives that may be found in nearly any well-outfitted knife kit. As you continue to learn more about cutting and cooking, you may want or need to acquire some highly specialized knives and cutting tools, such as those used almost exclusively in the bakeshop or butcher shop.

General-Purpose Knives

General-purpose knives can perform more than one function. Paring knives are considered general purpose because you can use them to trim or peel vegetables, and for a variety of cutting, chopping, mincing, and slicing tasks. As more and more Eastern-style knives are finding their way into knife kits and kitchens around the world, we've expanded our list here to include a number of general purpose Eastern-style knives, along with the traditional Western-style general-purpose knives: the chef's knife, utility knife, and paring knife. (See photos on pages 12 and 15.)

Chef's Knife A chef's knife (also known as a French knife) is the most often used item in any knife kit. It is designed and manufactured for wide-ranging general use in the kitchen. The blade is shaped and worked so that it can peel and trim, slice, chop, mince, fillet fish, and fabricate meats and poultry. In the hands of a skilled professional, this knife can be used to perform the tasks of many special-purpose knives.

The blade of a chef's knife typically ranges from 8 to 12 inches in length and is about 1½ to 2 inches wide at the heel or bolster, tapering to a point at the tip. When viewed from above, the spine should also appear to taper from its thickest point, at the bolster, toward the tip.

One sign of quality in a knife is the balance between the blade and the handle. Most good chef's knives are equally balanced, with the weight of the blade equal to the weight of the handle. Some knives have heavier blades than handles to give them additional weight and force for heavy-duty tasks like chopping through bones or heavy rinds. Some knives have most of the weight in the handle; this is typically true of knives used for fine work, for instance, a filleting knife or a paring knife.

The handle and the blade should join in such a way that you can chop foods on a cutting board without bashing your knuckles into the cutting surface. If possible, use a chef's knife to cut something before you buy it to determine which style of knife feels best and gives the best results.

The blade of the chef's knife has several distinct work areas: the tip, the cutting edge, the heel, the spine, and the flat of the blade.

The tip is used for fine work such as paring, trimming, and peeling. It can also be used to core fruits and vegetables or to score items so that they will marinate or cook more evenly.

The cutting edge is used for slicing tasks, such as cutting fish fillets into portions or carving cooked foods into slices. Cutting foods into neat dice, julienne, paysanne, and other precision cuts is easiest when you let the middle portion of the blade's long, sharp, cutting edge do the work.

The heel area of the blade is best suited to cutting tasks that require some force because the blade is the widest and the thickest at that point. The bolster is located at the heel of the blade, just where the handle and blade meet. The added heft provides the greatest possible concentration of weight and force at that spot in the blade. This permits you to chop through tendons and joints using a quick, sharp motion, or to slice through a winter squash's tough rind.

Even the parts of the blade without an edge have applications in the kitchen. The spine can be used to lightly score foods before pounding or butterflying them, or to crack lobster claws. The flat side of the blade can be used to crush garlic or to lift foods up from the cutting surface.

OPPOSITE, CLOCKWISE FROM TOP LEFT Three Asian-style cleavers (Chinese, *usuba, daido*), *yo-deba,* bird's beak (tourné), paring knife, clam knife, pizza wheel, pastry wheel, cheese-cutting tools (heart-shaped blade, bell-shape, serving fork, slicer), paring knife (ceramic blade), *santoku* (ceramic blade), and mezzaluna (CENTER).

Asian-Style Cleavers The Chinese-style cleaver has a blade that is rectangular in shape with a single-sided edge. The cleaver is used for a wide range of kitchen operations, including fine work such as peeling, trimming, and mincing, and for more demanding tasks including disjointing poultry or filleting fish. In addition to its usefulness as a knife, this style of cleaver can be used to tenderize meats by "chopping" them with the spine of the blade, to pound foods by flattening them with the broad side of the blade, and to transfer foods from the cutting board by using the blade as a bench scraper. For many Asian-trained chefs, and a growing number of Western-schooled chefs, this style of cleaver is the most important general-purpose knife they have in their kitchen or personal kit.

Gyuto (gi-yu-to) The *gyuto* is similar to a chef's knife. They can be slightly thinner than the average chef's knife and have Asian-style handles. This style of knife is not a traditional shape for Japanese knife makers; it is a double-edged knife and is rarely, if ever, available single-edged. It is used just as a chef's knife would be used.

Santoku (san-toe-koo) *Santoku* translates literally as "three virtues," according to Korin's *The Japanese Chef Knife Collection*. The name is derived from the practice of using this knife to cut meat, chicken, or pork (normally a specialty knife would be used for each item). This is a new multipurpose knife in the Japanese market, and has become extremely popular across the world. The shape is similar to a chef's knife, but the blade is shorter, as though the chef's knife had been compressed.

Utility Knife This smaller version of a chef's knife is used for light cutting, slicing, and peeling chores. The blade is generally 5 to 7 inches long. Not only is the blade shorter than that of a chef's knife, it is also thinner and lighter, making it useful for slicing smaller items such as tomatoes.

Usuba (oo-su-bah), Kamagata Usuba (kah-mah-gah-tah oo-su-bah), and Nakiri (nah-kee-ree) These three knives, made in Japan, are used for chopping vegetables. All three feature long, thin, narrow blades perfect for slicing, trimming, and chopping a variety of vegetables.

The traditional shape of the *usuba* and *nakiri* reflects the knife-making style known as *Kanto* that is favored by knife makers in Tokyo. These two knives have a long rectangular shape, like a longer, narrower cleaver. The difference between the two is that the *usuba* has a single-edged blade while the *nakiri* is double-edged.

The *kamagata usuba* is made in a style called *Kansai* that is preferred by knife makers in Osaka. The blade curves in from the spine to the tip and is single-edged.

Paring Knife Paring knives are the second most often used knife. This knife, used primarily for paring and trimming vegetables and fruits, has a 2- to 4-inch blade. Some blades taper to a point, much like a chef's knife; others have a curve or bend at the tip, sometimes referred to as a Granny knife. This knife is a frequently used item that you should take as much time to select as you do to choose your chef's knife.

A tourné knife is similar in size to a paring knife, but the blade is curved to make cutting the rounded surfaces of tournéed vegetables easier. The inverted curve of the blade gives this knife its second name, bird's beak.

Slicers Slicers have long, thin, narrow blades in order to make smooth slices in a single stroke. The type of edge on the blade is selected to make a particular food easier to slice. Some blades are quite flexible and others are rigid, depending upon the food they are used to slice. The tip of the slicer can be pointed or rounded.

Meat slicers are typically 15 to 18 inches long or longer, with taper ground or hollow-ground edges and relatively rigid blades. Salmon slicers, used for smoked salmon or gravlax, are even thinner than meat slicers and often have a granton edge to keep the moist, delicate flesh from sticking and tearing as it is sliced. These slicers generally have flexible blades. Slicers used for tomatoes, breads, or pastries are often serrated, scalloped, or saw-toothed.

LEFT TO RIGHT *Yo-deba* (butchering), *yanagi* (sushi and slicing), Western-style filleting knife (flexible blade), *sujihiki* (slicing and carving), *honesuki* (poultry butchering), scimitar (butchering), *hankotsu* (boning), and Western-style boning knife (rigid blade).

Knives for Butchering and Fabricating

Preparing meats, poultry, and fish in the professional kitchen calls for more specialized knives than the general-purpose knives just introduced. Their distinctive blade shapes make them easy to distinguish from a general-purpose knife. Their blades may be thin, narrow, flexible, or have some other unique characteristic, such as the pronounced curve of a scimitar, that sets them apart and improves their ability to perform one specific function. At minimum, most chefs have a boning knife and a filleting knife. If you are planning to do a lot of butchering, you may also need a scimitar and a butcher's cleaver.

Boning Knife A boning knife is used to separate raw meat from the bone. The blade—about 6 inches long—is thinner and shorter than the blade of a typical chef's knife and is usually rigid. Some boning knives have an upward curve; others are straight. The blade is narrower than a chef's knife blade to make it easier to work around bones, between muscle groups, and under gristle and the tough, shiny membrane called silverskin. Even if you use your boning knife less frequently than your chef's knife, you should still look for a high-quality boning knife with good stability and durability.

Filleting Knife Chef's knives and boning knives can be used to fillet fish, but these larger and more rigid blades often leave behind the flesh closest to the bone. Filleting knives are specifically designed for filleting fish. This knife is similar in shape and size to a boning knife, but has a more flexible blade. This permits you to separate the delicate flesh of a fish from the bones easily, with little loss of edible fish.

Deba, Yo-Deba (day-bah, yo-de-bah) The *deba* and *yo-deba* are butchering knives, used for breaking down both meats and fish. The *deba* has a single-edged blade, while the *yo-deba* has a Western-style double-edged blade. The blade shape is reminiscent of a chef's knife, but is much thicker. The weight and thickness of the blade make it ideal for chopping through bones and slicing through joints of meat and poultry.

The knife performs well when filleting fish for sashimi, but you may not get as high a yield as you would using a filleting knife. When preparing fish for sushi, the cleanness of the cut is most important, and the fish is usually further trimmed after it has been filleted—so yield is not necessarily as much of a concern.

Butcher's Cleavers Cleavers have a rectangular blade (the edge may be curved or straight, depending upon intended use). The blade is typically double-edged and is quite hefty, since it must cut through bones, joints, and tendons. The cleaver is used for very heavy cutting tasks in the butcher shop. Once those cuts are made, the chef switches to either a scimitar or a boning knife to slice through the meat.

Scimitar The long, curved blade of a scimitar makes it well suited to the slicing action required to cut through large cuts of raw meat when portioning them into steaks, cutlets, or medallions. The blade can range in length from 12 to 16 inches.

BELOW, CLOCKWISE FROM LEFT Fish scaler, lobster cracker, scissors (shears) and string, meat mallet (tenderizer), meat pounder (for cutlets, etc.), straight trussing needed, angled trussing needle, barding needle, shrimp peeler and deveiner, and tweezers.

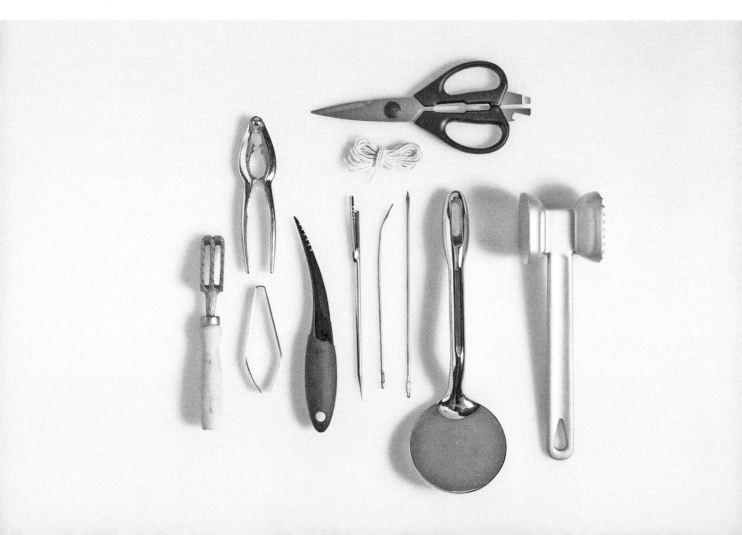

Clam and Oyster Knives Clam knives have a 3- to 4-inch-long blade with a rounded tip and a handle. Oyster knives have a short, pointed blade with a guard at the point where the handle meets the blade. The different shapes represent the different ways that these two mollusks are opened. To open a clam, slip the edge of the blade between the shells on the edge opposite the hinge. To open an oyster, press the pointed tip of the blade into the hinge. Once the knife has penetrated the shell, the blade is twisted to release the shells.

Follow these safety precautions when using shellfish knives:

» **Wear a mesh glove to avoid puncturing your hand with the knife blade.**

» **Keep a watch for shells that splinter; bits of shell can lodge in the meat.**

» **Wear goggles to protect your eyes.**

Specialty Knives

Over time, special knives have been designed to handle special cutting tasks. Cheese knives and tools with circular blades, such as pizza or dough cutters, all fill a special cutting need.

Cheese Knives There are a variety of cheese knives, each designed specifically for a particular type of cheese.

Hard cheese knives generally have a flat cutting surface and textured or etched sides on the blade to slice against the cheese evenly while preventing the cheese from sticking to the sides. Some knives have holes to make it easier to slice soft or crumbly cheeses.

Parmesean knives are specially designed to break up Parmesan or similar hard grating cheeses. Shaped like a heart, the blade tapers to a sharp point that can pierce the rind and the hard, dry cheese. To remove chunks of cheese, sink the blade into the cheese, driving it about ½ to 1 inch into the cheese, and then, with a twist of your wrist, you can pry off a piece.

Blue-cheese knives have 6-inch-long blades shaped like a bell to cut and spread any soft or crumbly cheese. Some general-purpose cheese slicers have a granton edge, while the blades of other cheese slicers may have holes, so the cheese won't stick or rip, or they may have a serrated edge. You may also find cheese slicers that have a pronged tip, to make it easier to transfer the cheese to a plate after you cut it.

Double-handled knives allow you to put your weight into the cut. These knives are ideal for breaking down larger blocks of hard cheeses. The blades can reach up to 13 inches in length.

Dough Cutters (Pizza Cutters) This style of cutter can be used to cut pizza, of course, but it is also valuable for cutting a variety of pastries and doughs. It can make long, even cuts with no ragged edges. A circular blade is mounted on an axle. As you push the cutter over the item you want to cut, the blade turns, like a wheel. Smaller cutters are used to cut pastry doughs. Some cutters have fluted edges; ravioli cutters are an example. Specially produced dough cutters, such as a croissant cutter, can cut many smaller pieces from a large sheet of dough at one time.

Mezzaluna The name *mezzaluna*, or half moon, reflects the crescent shape of the blade. Both ends of the blade are joined to a handle. Some versions have two blades parallel to each other. To use a mezzaluna, rock the blade back and forth over whatever you are cutting (typically fresh herbs, garlic, or greens) to chop or mince them as coarse or fine as you need them to be.

Although a mezzaluna can be used on a flat surface such as a typical cutting board, it is traditionally paired with either a cutting board that has a concave area or a wooden bowl to make the most of the curved cutting surface.

Sharpening and Honing Tools

No knife kit can be considered complete without sharpening and honing tools, because the key to the proper and efficient use of any knife is making sure that it stays sharp. (Instructions for sharpening and honing knives can be found on pages 42–49.) Knife blades are given an edge on a sharpening stone and maintained between sharpenings by honing with a steel.

TOP ROW, LEFT TO RIGHT Flat steel with a ribbed surface, oval flat steel, round steel, diamond steel, ceramic steel, Arkansas triple-mount stone, Carborundum stone set in a wood base, Carborundum stone; BOTTOM ROW ceramic stone (right), water stone (left).

Whetstones

A whetstone is a block of hard material, synthetic or natural, that is used to whet, or grind and sharpen, a blade.

Stones are available in a variety of sizes, textures, and materials. Sharpening stones are produced from such man-made and natural materials as Carborundum, silicon carbide, aluminum oxide, ceramic, whetstone, industrial diamond, and naturally occurring sandstone or Arkansas stone—a hard stone quarried from the Ozark Mountains.

The relative coarseness or fineness of the stone's material is referred to as its grit. A coarse grit grinds away more of the blade, useful when knives are very dull or when they have notches. A very fine grit means that the stone will remove less of the blade itself but will result in a smoother, sharper edge.

Large stones—some with several sides and a reservoir for lubricating oil—have the advantage of accommodating large and heavy blades. Smaller stones may be a bit difficult to use on longer knives but are much easier to transport.

All stones need some sort of lubrication as you work your knife. The type of lubrication you choose depends on the stone and your personal preference. Regardless of the type of lubricant you choose, stones do wear over time, developing a concave or hollowed surface. "Stone fixers," or flattening stones, can be scraped against the sharpening surface to smooth and even out the face of the stone.

Sharpening stones fall into four basic categories: water stones, oil stones, ceramic stones, and diamond stones.

Water Stones

Water stones are composed of a compressed, granular material that soaks up water like a sponge. They are meant to be soaked in water for at least 10 minutes before you sharpen your knife. This softens the stone and allows it to form a paste as you work your knife's edge across the surface, flushing out the old grit and exposing clean grit. Water stones are available with either a single-size grit or as a combination stone.

The advantage of using a water stone is that the grit is often much finer than on other stones, so you can get a good edge on your knife more quickly than with other stones.

One disadvantage is that water stones wear down more quickly than other stones. The stone can be flattened again by rubbing two stones together until the surfaces are flat, or by using a lapping tool that can scrape away the upper surface and uncover clean grit.

Oil Stones

Oil stones are made from either natural or synthetic materials. An Arkansas stone and flint are natural stones. Man-made oil stones are most commonly made of aluminum oxide (sometimes known as India stones) or silicon carbide.

The hardness of a natural stone correlates to grit in a synthetic stone. Soft Arkansas stones act like coarse-grit synthetic stones and hard Arkansas stones are equivalent to fine-grit synthetic stones. Hard Arkansas stones are made from a novaculite, a black or white stone that is almost pure silica. Translucent Arkansas stones are the hardest and are used for finishing the edge, in the same way that a fine-grit synthetic stone is employed to refine your knife's edge.

An individual stone consists of a single hardness. To make sharpening your knives on Arkansas stones more efficient, you may prefer to use a triple-mounted holder for three different stones and three different hardnesses.

Choose a food-grade oil to use on your stone, but you should not use cooking or eating oils on your stone because those oils will turn rancid. Mineral oil is a good common choice. Apply a thin coating of the oil to the stone before you sharpen your knife. You can also use water as the lubricant for an oil stone (but remember to never put oil on a water stone).

Ceramic Stone

Ceramic stones are a type of manufactured stone. They are extremely hard and, unlike water stones, require only a light film of water when you sharpen your knife. Some people simply spray or mist the stone as they work. Ceramic stones have another advantage over water stones—they are far less messy.

Ceramic stones are available in a variety of grits. They are more expensive and only have a single-size grit per stone. They work as quickly as a water stone but wear down even more slowly than oil stones. A good ceramic stone could last a lifetime.

Diamond Stones

These stones are, in fact, plates of steel with diamond crystals embedded in the surface. Different sizes and amounts of crystals determine the grit. These stones sharpen knife edges quickly and although they don't wear as other stones do, the crystals smooth out and get dull over time. The biggest disadvantage of diamond stones is their cost.

Steels

Steels, like sharpening stones, are available in coarse, medium, and fine grits. They may be round, oval, or flat. The length of the steel's working surface can range from 3 inches for a pocket version to over 14 inches. The easiest and safest length for a steel is at least 2 to 3 inches longer than the blade of your chef's knife.

Hard steel is the traditional material for steels. Other materials such as glass, ceramic, and diamond-impregnated surfaces are also available. Those made of metal are magnetic, which helps the blade retain proper alignment and also collects metal shavings. Ceramic and diamond-impregnated steels are not magnetic.

A guard or hilt between the steel and the handle protects the user, and a ring on the bottom of the handle can be used to hang the steel.

Electric Knife Sharpeners

Most electric sharpeners use a rapidly rotating abrasive surface that wears away the knife's damaged edge to form a new, sharper edge. The abrasive surface can be a belt, wheel, or series of disks.

Because they operate at high speeds, there is a danger of over-sharpening the blade. Even a short time in an electric sharpener can grind away too much of the blade, causing excessive wear and significantly shorten the knife's useful life.

If your kitchen has an electric knife sharpener, be sure to get clear instructions on how to use the sharpener for the best possible results and the least damage to your knife.

Additional Hand Tools

A number of cutting tools are used in the kitchen. Some of these tools make large-volume work easier, faster, and more efficient. Others are used to perform very specific cutting tasks. The tools covered in this section are used to slice, dice, cut, shred, or grate foods, as well as to trim or manipulate foods as they cook.

Ice-Carving Tools

Large and small ice carvings are used for both display and individual service. Carvers today sculpt mirror images into the ice, pack it with snow, and create a white-on-clear display that looks almost like a holograph. Less-demanding displays are easy to make from a split block of ice that sandwiches a logo.

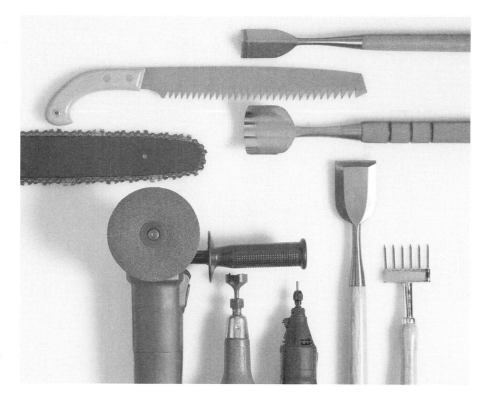

FROM TOP V-shaped chisel, handsaw, half-moon chisel, chain saw; FROM LEFT sander, power drills (showing two different heads), flat chisel, and chipper.

TOP ROW Nested ring biscuit cutters, spider, spaetzle maker; CENTER ROW dough docker, garlic press, cherry or olive pitter, microplane, ripple-cut slicer; BOTTOM ROW citrus reamer, paddle for spaetzle, and egg slicer.

Tongs and Similar Tools

Chefs use tongs the way they might use their thumb and forefinger: to grip something firmly enough to lift or turn it. Other tools similar in basic function that you might find in a chef's personal tool kit include some less-obvious options: tweezers or forceps, pliers, and specialized tools for cracking nuts or lobster shells.

Tongs Tongs are available in a variety of sizes. The two sides of the tongs are joined at one end with a hinge. A spring keeps the tongs open and provides resistance as you clamp them together. Some have a locking mechanism that holds the tongs closed until the lock is released. The gripping end may be rounded with a scalloped edge. In addition to their obvious use to lift and turn foods in a pan, deep-fat fryer, or on the grill, chefs often use tongs instead of their bare fingers to test the doneness of a food. By pressing the tongs against the food, they can feel how soft or firm the food is.

Tweezers and Forceps Tweezers and forceps are very useful in the kitchen for removing small bones from fish or removing foods from jars with long or narrow necks. Forceps look like scissors but they lock into place, so you don't have to worry about losing your hold on something as you move it. Tweezers are small enough to use for very fine or delicate work. Anyone responsible for displaying foods attractively, whether a banquet or garde manger chef or a food stylist, typically has a number of different tweezers of all different sizes and shapes.

Pliers, nut crackers, and seafood crackers are used for heavier tasks that require a bit of force, such as crushing a shell so that the edible portion can be picked out. Needle-nose pliers are often used to remove bones from fish—especially the pin bones found in salmon fillets.

Scissors and Shears

Scissors are part of any kitchen's equipment. They are used to cut parchment paper, open packaging, cut grapes into clusters, trim and mince herbs, and cut string. They are also useful to cut through small bones and shells. (See photo on page 20.)

Shears are larger, sturdier scissors, used to cut through heavier items. Poultry shears can cut through the tight joints and ligaments of chickens, ducks, and geese. Shears may have a textured edge on the blades. Poultry shears come apart at the joint for easy cleaning and sharpening. In the kitchen, it is important to use shears stamped with the National Safety Foundation's (NSF) mark.

Spatulas

The term *spatula* derives from the same Greek root word that gave us "sword," "spoon," and "spade." A spatula consists of a relatively broad, flat head or blade with a handle.

Some spatuas are used to turn or lift foods as they cook—for instance, pancakes or hamburgers. The blade of a spatula may be perforated or solid. (A fish spatula is a specific type of spatula with a wedge-shaped, slotted head that is smaller and more flexible than the standard "pancake" turner.) They may have an offset blade, to make it easier to reach into pans. Others have straight blades; these spatulas are similar to palette knives and sandwich spreaders.

Another type of spatula has a flexible head made of rubber or silicon that you may hear referred to as a rubber scraper. The head can be constructed from rubber, silicon, and heat-resistant materials, making them suitable for use in hot pans. Handles are often made of nonconductive materials such as plastic or wood. These spatulas are used to fold batters, spread soft foods, and scrape out the contents of pans, bowls, and containers cleanly.

Peelers

A peeler removes the outer skin of a fruit or vegetable. There are two basic kinds of peelers: a rotary peeler, with a swiveling, vertical head; and a stationary peeler, with a horizontal head. After using the blade to slice away the skin or peel, the tip is used to remove any blemishes, spots, or the eyes from fresh fruits and vegetables.

A good peeler should have two features: There should be a cutting surface on each side of the split head, allowing it to peel in both directions; and a well-constructed peeler will have a removable blade for easy cleaning and replacement.

Graters and Rasps

Graters and rasps are used to shred and grate items. Box graters have four sides with openings of different sizes and shapes on each side. The smaller the hole, the finer the end result. The finest side is used for grating and should be used with firm or hard textured foods (such as nutmeg or Parmesan cheese). The larger openings are used to shred foods with a moderately firm texture (such as Cheddar or mozzarella cheese, carrots, or zucchini). Some graters will have a slicing side, ideal for cheese or firm fruits. Some graters will have a section on one side with flower-like openings used to grating nutmeg and make citrus zest.

Nutmeg graters have a curved surface and small openings. Graters for hard cheese, such as the Mouli grater, have a drum pierced with holes that turns against the food and cuts into it.

For large-volume work, grating attachments are available for mixers, grinders, food choppers, and food processors.

Rasps, such as microplanes or nutmeg graters, are handheld graters and come in a variety of textured openings, similar to box graters. They are used for the same purposes as graters and achieve the same results.

Graters should be washed and rinsed immediately after use. To clean the grating sides, soak the grater in clean soapy water or spray with water to force out any particles of food. Running a sponge over the cutting side of the grate will simply shred the sponge and clog the openings in the grater.

Corers, Wedgers, and Pitters

Corers remove the core of a fruit without damaging the skin or integrity of the whole fruit. They are hollow, sharp-edged cylinders attached to a short handle. To use them, position the open end of the corer over the core. Push the corer into the fruit, twisting it as you push. Once you've pushed the corer completely through the fruit, pull it back out, removing the core.

An apple wedger is used to core and cut an apple into even slices, all at the same time. It is a metal ring, with handles on opposite sides, and it contains a series of sharp-edged slats that connect to a smaller, inner circle. The design resembles a bicycle wheel but with fewer spokes.

Olive and cherry pitters have a small rod that you push into the food to force the pit out. One common pitter design resembles pliers, with a rounded bowl at one side to hold the cherry or olive and the rod on the other side. When you squeeze the pitter, the rod plunges into the food and pushes the pit out. Another pitter design available resembles the plunger end of a hypodermic needle, with a spring-loaded mechanism that you push down with your thumb to force the pit out.

Zesters and Channel Knives

Zesters remove the flavorful, colored peel of citrus fruit without cutting into the white, bitter pith. The head resembles a small metal hand with small, sharp-edged rings in place of fingers. The zester cuts away thin strips from a food, generally fruit or vegetables, as it is scraped along the surface.

Channel knives are used to score the skin or rind of vegetables or fruit and for other decorative cuts. You can use a channel knife to cut long strips from oranges or lemons. The cutting surface is a small indentation at the edge of a teardrop-shaped metal head.

Mandolines and Benriners

Mandolines and benriners create slices, bâtons, juliennes, and gauffrettes (or waffle cuts). They are most appropriate when you need to produce a large volume because they are quick, efficient, and consistent.

The French-style mandoline is made of nickel-plated stainless steel with blades of high-carbon steel. Levers adjust the blades to achieve the cut and thickness desired. There is a carriage device that holds the food and a hand guard that permits you to press the food firmly against the blade without fear of cutting yourself. There are folding legs that can be adjusted and locked into place before working to make cutting easier and safer. The legs are folded beneath the device for storage.

The ideal mandoline's blades are adjustable. By adjusting a lever on the back of the mandoline, you can lock different blades into place. Some have inserts to produce a variety of specialty cuts, including fluted slices, wavy or crinkle-cut sticks, or gauffrettes.

Cleaning and maintaining the device is as simple as rinsing it with running warm or hot water and scrubbing with soap, if necessary, to remove food particles. Be careful of the cutting surfaces and inserts, as they are extremely sharp. Dry the device by hand or allow it to air-dry; its stainless-steel construction is rust-proof. Because of the moving parts, it might be necessary to lubricate joints occasionally. Apply the lubricant carefully, keeping it away from the cutting surface, where it would come into contact with food.

A tool similar to the mandoline, known as a Japanese-style mandoline or benriner, is also widely used in both professional and home kitchens. The blade is made of stainless steel, but the rest of the cutter is made of plastic, making it less expensive than the traditional mandoline. The main blade should be adjustable, and it can have interchangeable blades as well.

Ripple Cutters

Special cutters or blades are required to produce ripple cuts. Hand tools and slicers are available for this purpose. The ripple-cut blade on a mandoline is used to cut cucumbers, carrots, potatoes, and soft-skinned squashes. Special blades are also available for use with food processors, slicers, and choppers.

Guitars (Egg Cutters)

The cutting tool known as a *guitar* got its name because the cutting wires look like the strings of a guitar. They have of a number of parallel wires set into a frame or between two handles. You cut food with a guitar either by pressing the food onto the wires, which make slices as thick as the spaces between the wires, or by pressing the guitar onto the food. Egg cutters are also a type of guitar. Some egg cutters are made in two halves, held together by a hinge. You set the food you want to cut on one side of the egg cutter, then close the cutter to slice the food. Egg cutters, despite their name, can be used to slice other relatively firm foods, such as avocados or mushrooms.

Food Mill

This kitchen tool purées soft foods while at the same time removing seeds, skin, and fibers by hand-cranking a flat, curved blade over a disk. This action both chops food and forces it out of the small holes of the strainer, giving the product a rustic, puréed texture without liquefying it like a blender or food processor might. Most professional models have interchangeable disks with holes of varying fineness. An exception is the Foley food mill, which has a mesh disk that is fitted into place. A food mill should come apart for easier cleaning. Each piece should be cleaned separately and dried; then the machine may be reassembled and stored.

Ricer

This is a device in which cooked food, often potatoes, is placed in a pierced, hinged hopper. A plate at the end of a lever pushes the food through the openings in the hopper. (Garlic presses and french-fry cutters operate on the same principle.) This achieves a roughly puréed texture, similar to a food mill. Ricers do not come apart at the hinge, so when you clean them, make sure that you remove any food particles. Dry the ricer thoroughly, especially around the hinge, before storing it.

Garlic Press

Used to crush cloves of garlic and make small quantities of garlic paste, garlic presses are similar in concept to ricers, only smaller. A pierced hopper holds the clove of garlic and a plunger is pressed against the clove, forcing it through the small openings.

Carving and Kitchen Forks

Forks are used to steady foods as they are cut, to test the doneness of braised meats, and to hold and serve slices of carved meat. Kitchen forks are long, two-pronged forks that have flat heads and long tines. Carving forks have curved heads and are more visually appealing for use in front of customers.

Parisienne Scoops

Parisienne scoops are designed to scoop out balls or ovals (depending on the shape of the scoop) from fruits and vegetables. The scoops are made in a range of sizes and may be round, oval, fluted, or smooth. Besides making attractive balls of food, these scoops can core fruits and vegetables for presentation. You can scrape the scoop down the length of a zucchini to hollow it out, stuff it, and make zucchini boats, for example.

Wire Mesh Gloves

Mesh gloves are used to protect your hands in situations where you may not have as much control over a blade, such as a mandoline, electric slicer, or a clam or oyster knife. These gloves are made of a series of linked or woven rings that resembles medieval chain mail.

Reamers

A reamer is a ridged cone with a handle that is used to juice citrus efficiently. It can be made from plastic, wood, or various other substances, but plastic is ideal because it is less likely to absorb juice, bacteria, and oils that can stain wood.

Meat Pounders and Meat Tenderizers

A pounder or tenderizer is composed of a weighted head—textured or flat, round or square—attached to a handle. Any of these metal or wood tools can be used to pound meats to make them thinner or an even thickness so that the pieces cook more quickly and evenly. Make sure the tool has an NSF logo on it; otherwise it may be unsafe to use in the kitchen. (See photo on page 20.)

Shrimp Deveiners

Shaped like a curved, elongated teardrop, the thin "nose" of a shrimp deveiner is inserted along the digestive track of a shrimp, and, with a clean jerk, removes both the vein and the shell. They are usually made of plastic, and are inexpensive and easy to clean. There are various types, and not all are made of plastic. Regardless of construction, a sturdy nose is the key; a flimsy nose can break off easily. (See photo on page 20.)

Large Cutting Tools

Large pieces of equipment with moving blades can be extremely dangerous if they are not used with understanding and respect. The importance of observing all the necessary safety precautions cannot be overemphasized. To keep large equipment functioning properly and to prevent injury or accident, you must keep the equipment properly maintained and cleaned. As these tools are essential for a number of operations, you should be able to use them with confidence.

Using Large Cutting Equipment Safely

Observe the following guidelines when working with large equipment:

1. Obtain proper instruction on the machine's safe operation. Do not be afraid to ask for extra help.

2. First turn off and then unplug electrical equipment before assembling or breaking down the equipment.

3. Use all safety features. Be sure that lids are secure, hand guards are used, and the machine is stable.

4. Clean and sanitize the equipment thoroughly after each use.

5. Be sure that all pieces of equipment are properly reassembled and left unplugged after each use.

6. Report any problems or malfunctions promptly and alert coworkers to the problem (an "out of order" sign attached to the machine itself is a good approach).

Food Processor

A food processor is a machine that houses the motor separately from the bowl, blades, and lid. Food processors can grind, purée, blend, emulsify, crush, knead, and, with special disks, slice, julienne, and shred foods.

Electric Slicer

This machine is used to slice foods to even thickness. A carrier moves the food back and forth against a circular blade, which is generally carbon steel. There may be separate motors to operate the carrier and the blade. To avoid injury, all the safety features incorporated in a food slicer, especially the hand guard, should be used.

Meat Grinder

This is a freestanding machine or an attachment for a standing mixer. A meat grinder generally has a feed tray and a food pusher (also known as a tamper) and should have dies of varying sizes.

The foods should be cut in a size and shape that allows them to drop easily through the feed tube and into the opening only as quickly as the machine can handle them. The tamper should be used only to free foods that stick to the tray or the mouth of the feed tube; it should not be used to force foods down the feed tube.

All food contact areas should be kept scrupulously clean and well chilled. This is important not only for sanitation and wholesome food but also to produce the best possible texture in the finished dish.

Vertical Chopping Machine (VCM)

This machine operates on the same principle as a blender. A motor at the base is permanently attached to a bowl with integral blades. As a safety precaution, the hinged lid must be locked in place before the unit will operate. The VCM is used to whip, emulsify, blend, or crush foods.

Food Chopper (Buffalo Chopper)

Generally made of aluminum with a stainless-steel bowl, food choppers are available in floor and tabletop models. The food is placed in a rotating bowl that passes under a hood, where blades chop the food. Some units have hoppers or feed tubes and interchangeable disks for slicing and grating. Food choppers are sometimes called buffalo choppers because, viewed in profile, they look a little like a buffalo.

KNIFE SKILLS

2

Learning to use a knife properly is similar to learning to write your

name. At first, you concentrate on holding the pencil. You have to stop and remember how to wrap your fingers around it. Instead of actually writing, you begin by making individual letters, shaping each one carefully and deliberately. As you continue to practice, writing your own name becomes an automatic activity, because you write it so often. Today, when you sign a document, you don't think about how you are holding your writing instrument, nor do you consciously shape each letter.

Most of us learn to write in a classroom. Although penmanship is taught in the same way at the same time to a whole class of students, each individual has a unique way of writing. You learn first to hold a knife and to make basic cuts following basic guidelines and instruction first. Then, with practice, you learn to hold your knife and perform cuts in a way that suits your physiology, temperament, and working style.

Eventually, you should acquire both accuracy and speed, but it is not expected that you will have both as you start out. As with writing, your primary goal is to be as accurate and precise as possible, even if you aren't working at lightning speed. By concentrating on accuracy at first, and not worrying about speed, your deep knowledge of making the various cuts will lead naturally to increased confidence and speed.

Knife Selection

A knife that fits your hand and is in prime cutting condition feels like a natural part of your hand. The right knife for you depends upon several different factors, including the work you plan to do with the knife, the amount of time it will be in your hand on any given day, and the amount of money you have to spend. Your knives should fit your hand. A handle that is too big for your hand is a sign of a knife that you will find hard to control with precision and ease. A handle that is too small may force you to use an awkward grip that is fatiguing.

Knives should feel substantial in your hand but not too heavy. You may prefer a heavy knife for some tasks and a lighter knife for others. Another factor to consider is how well balanced it feels as you hold it. The weight should feel evenly distributed between the handle and the blade.

Be sure to take the time to hold knives and, if possible, use them to cut something before you make the decision to buy a knife. Knives can be expensive. They represent an investment in your career, so give the purchasing process time and plenty of thought.

What's In Your Knife Kit?

"All chefs love to collect knives. Each one is a little trophy, a souvenir. I have a knife that my first chef gave me that makes thinner slices than any other knife I own. And another that I bought on a camping trip in Canada has a blade with an unusual curve that's perfect for working with fruits.

Don't be fooled by the number of knives a chef acquires over a lifetime of cooking. You don't really need dozens of knifes. In fact, all chefs have a favorite, the one knife they never want to be without. That's the knife that feels like it was made for their grip, the knife that takes a good edge. The one with a blade that fits their cutting style and a heft that feels perfect matched to their strengths. The one they can use for nearly anything, from peeling a ripe peach to cutting up a chicken to dicing an onion.

Finding the right knife can take time. I probably 'test drove' at least 10 different brands before I found the knife for me. I went to large stores, small stores. I asked for suggestions. Buying a chef's knife is personal.

Once you find a knife that you like, you need to practice until your skills are as habitual as driving your car or dialing your phone. Practicing gives you skill. Skill gives you confidence. Confidence puts you on the road to mastery."

CHEF MARK AINSWORTH, THE CULINARY INSTITUTE OF AMERICA

» **Always hold a knife by its handle.**

» **Never attempt to catch a falling knife.**

» **Never borrow a knife without asking permission, and always return it promptly when you are finished using it.**

» **When passing a knife to someone else, lay it down on a work surface and allow the other person to pick it up, or pass it handle first (the handle extended to the person receiving the knife).**

» **Do not allow the blade of a knife to extend over the edge of a table or cutting board.**

» **Do not use knives to open bottles, loosen drawers, and so on.**

» **Do not leave knives loose in areas where they cannot easily be seen or wouldn't be found normally (under tables, on shelves, and similar spots).**

» **If you must carry an unsheathed knife in the kitchen, hold it straight down at your side with the sharp edge facing behind you.**

Handling and Maintaining Knives

You can always distinguish professional cooks and chefs by the care and attention they lavish on their tools. They keep their knife edges in top shape, honing them frequently as they work, sharpening them on stones, taking them to a knife smith when the edges need to be rebuilt, cradling them in sheaths before stowing them in a kit or drawer. No professional worth his or her salt would dream of dropping a knife into a pot sink or putting a knife away dirty.

Professional pride certainly plays a part in this behavior. More to the point, however, is the professional's sure knowledge that a knife is only valuable as long as it is properly maintained. A well-cared-for knife can make cutting tasks easier to perform. A sharp knife does not require as much effort as a dull one; you really can let the knife cut the food. Clean knives will not contaminate wholesome foods, clean cutting surfaces, or knife kits. They are easier to hold without fear of losing your grip. Knives that are washed by hand don't get chipped or broken under the weight of heavy pots or damaged by the intense heat and chemicals of a dishwasher.

If you have selected your knives carefully, and purchased the best quality knife for the job at hand, you can keep those knives in peak condition by:

» **learning and observing the basic rules of knife safety and etiquette**
» **mastering techniques for honing on a steel and sharpening on a stone**
» **using the appropriate cutting surface**
» **cleaning and sanitizing knives as you work**
» **storing knives properly**

Sharpening Knives on a Stone

Sharpening stones are used to sharpen the edge once it has grown dull through ordinary use. Like many other techniques in the professional kitchen, there is some disagreement over what constitutes the "right" way. Opinion is split about whether your knife blade should be run over a stone from heel to tip or tip to heel. Similarly, some chefs prefer to use a lubricant such as mineral oil on their stones, while others swear by water. Most chefs do agree, however, that consistency in the direction of the stroke used to pass the blade over the stone is important. Once you find the method that suits you best, be sure to use the same technique every time.

General Sharpening Guidelines Despite the fact that chefs may have differing opinions about the type of stone or lubricant to use or the exact motion of the blade as it comes in contact with the stone, there are some aspects of proper knife sharpening that are agreed upon.

Allow yourself enough room to work. You should be able to move your arms without knocking things over or inadvertently jostling another worker.

Anchor the stone to keep it from slipping as you work. Place Carborundum or diamond stones on a dampened cloth or rubber mat or lock a triple-faced stone into position so that it cannot move.

Lubricate the stone with mineral oil or water. Water or mineral oil helps reduce friction as you sharpen your knife. The heat caused by friction may not seem significant, but it can eventually harm the blade. Be consistent about the type of lubricant you use on your stone.

Always sharpen the blade in the same direction. This ensures that the edge remains even and in proper alignment. We have illustrated two methods commonly used with sharpening stones, one in which the blade is sharpened from heel to tip, and a second in which the blade is sharpened working from tip to heel.

Begin sharpening the edge on the stone or the side of the stone with the coarsest grit you require. The duller the blade, the coarser the grit should be. Finish sharpening on the finest stone and wash the knife thoroughly before you use or store it.

Hold the knife at the correct angle as you work. A 20-degree angle is suitable for chef's knives and knives with similar blades. You may need to adjust the angle by a few degrees to properly sharpen thinner blades, such as slicers, or thicker blades, such as cleavers.

Make strokes of equal number and equal pressure on each side of the blade. Do not over-sharpen the edge on coarse stones. After about ten strokes on each side of the blade, move on to the next finer grit.

Method One calls for the knife to be drawn across the stone working from heel to tip. You are drawing it toward you as you work. Method Two calls for the knife to be drawn across the stone working from tip to heel. You are pushing it away from you as you work.

Method One for Sharpening Knives on a Stone

1. Arrange the stone so that it is parallel to the edge of your work surface. Hold the blade so that it makes a 20-degree angle with the surface of the stone. For this sharpening method, begin at the heel of the blade and begin to pull the blade toward you.

2. Run the entire edge over the surface of the stone, keeping the pressure on the knife even. At this stage, you are sharpening the part of the blade that gets the greatest amount of use. Continue to pull the blade over the stone in a smooth, fluid motion.

3. As you continue to pull the blade over the stone, you will eventually draw it completely off the stone. Do not press so hard on the blade that it slips out of control. Turn the blade over and repeat the process on the opposite side of the blade to sharpen the other side of a double-edged blade.

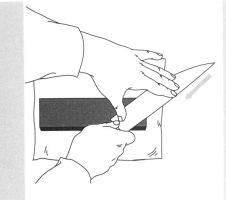

Keep the blade at a 20-degree angle (step 1).

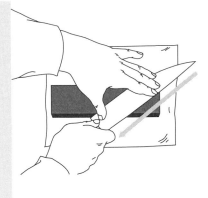

Use your fingertips to maintain steady pressure (step 2).

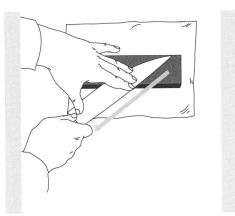

Finish at the tip. Repeat on other side (step 3).

Method Two for Sharpening Knives on a Stone

1. Arrange the stone on a damp cloth or rubber mat so that it is nearly perpendicular to the edge of your work surface, as shown in the accompanying illustrations. In this method, the tip of the knife comes in contact with the stone first. Notice that instead of using the tips of your thumb and three fingers, this method is easiest when you control the blade by putting three fingers on the flat side of the blade, fairly close together. The pad of your thumb rests against the spine of the knife to keep it stable.

2. Push the entire edge over the surface of the stone, keeping the blade's angle of contact consistent. If you have positioned your stone well, the edge will stay in contact with the stone over the entire length of the stone for an even, smooth edge.

3. Continue to maintain constant even pressure. As you push the blade off one side, shift the pressure from the fingers on the flat side of the blade to the hand holding the handle so you don't lose control. Turn the blade over and repeat the process once more on the opposite side of the blade to sharpen the other side of a double-edged blade.

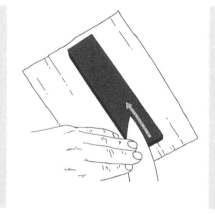

Start at the tip of the blade (step 1).

Push the blade over the stone (step 2).

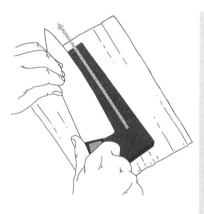

Finish the stroke smoothly (step 3).

Honing Knives on a Steel

Whenever you are using your knives, you should have a steel handy. Get into the habit of using a steel on your knives before you start cutting. Steels are not used to sharpen the edge; they are used to realign it because, with use, the edge starts to roll over to one side. With the variety of steels available today, you can easily find a steel that is comfortable in your hand. Maintaining your edge with a steel improves both the quality and the efficiency of all your knife work.

General Guidelines for Honing with a Steel

» **Allow yourself plenty of room as you work, and stand with your weight evenly distributed.**

» **Clean and dry your hands, the handle of the steel, and the handle of the knife. It is hard to maintain control over a slippery or wet tool. Hold the steel with your thumb and fingers tucked safely behind the guard.**

» **Use a light touch, stroking evenly and consistently. Lay the blade against the steel; don't slap it. Listen for a light ringing sound; a heavy, grinding sound indicates that you are applying too much pressure.**

» **Draw the blade along the steel so that the entire edge touches the steel. Work in the same direction on each side of the blade and each time you steel your knife to keep the edge straight.**

» **Be sure to keep the pressure even to avoid wearing away the metal in the center of the edge. Over time, this could produce a curve in the edge.**

» **Keep the knife blade at a 20-degree angle to the steel, the same angle you maintain when you sharpen the edge on a stone.**

» **If a blade requires more than five strokes per side on a steel, it probably should be sharpened on a stone.**

Shown on pages 48 and 49 are two methods for steeling knives. In Method One, both the knife and the steel are held in the air. It is safest to work so that the knife is pulled from the heel to the tip as you work. In Method Two, the steel is held with the tip kept in contact with a work surface. This makes it a little easier to maintain a consistent angle of contact between the knife and the steel. There are yet more techniques you may have an opportunity to learn. Whatever method you choose, the guidelines below will help you make effective use of your steel.

Professional Sharpening

Sometimes it is necessary to bring your knives to a professional sharpener. If your knives have become chipped or dull to such a degree that you can't bring back the edge on a stone, you can have the blade reground by a professional.

When you bring your knife to a smith, make sure they use the proper equipment. Some grinders have too coarse a grit and spin too quickly to properly sharpen the knife. They grinder will generate so much heat that it will ruin the blade. The heat will draw the hardness out of the knife, coloring the blade, and making it impossible for the knife to hold an edge again. Richard Von Husen, one of the owners of Warren Kitchen & Cutlery, which is located in Rhinebeck, New York, sharpens many of the knives belonging to the students and chefs of The Culinary Institute of America. He offers some insight about having a knife professionally sharpened:

We use belt sanders and grinding wheels to sharpen the knife, depending on the knife and how you hold it. Knives are usually started on slow-speed, wet grinding wheels. Buffing wheels are used to hone the final edge of the knife, after it is ground. If a knife needs a lot of work, you'd start it on a belt sander to remove material and reform the edge, then move on to the other machines.

We use a hollow grinding machine for hollow-ground blades. I would not recommend anyone taking their nicer knives to a service where they use hollow grinding equipment, unless the blade is hollow ground. You need to ask what kind of grinding equipment a service uses. It can be confusing today, because some knives have the granton edge with little hollows; that may be referred to as a hollowed edge, even though it isn't hollow ground. The hollow grinder is made up of two wheels that grind into the sides of the edge to produce two deep hollows instead of a "V."

RICHARD VON HUSEN, WARREN KITCHEN & CUTLERY, RHINEBECK, NY

Method One for Steeling

1. Hold the steel in your guiding hand and your knife in the hand you use for cutting. Grip the handles securely. As you begin, the steel is nearly horizontal and the knife is nearly vertical, with the heel of the blade resting on the steel's inner side.

2. Rotate your wrist to pull the blade's edge along the steel in a downward motion. The motion should be very smooth and rapid. Be sure that the blade makes 20-degree angle with the surface of the steel.

3. Continue to rotate your wrist while you finish the first stroke, pulling the tip of the knife smoothly off the steel. Keep the blade in contact with the steel throughout the entire stroke. Repeat the process, starting with the opposite side of the blade resting on the steel's outer side.

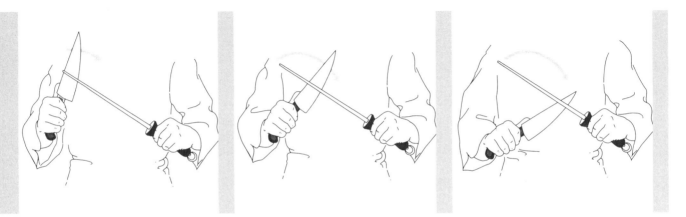

The blade rests on the steel's inner side (step 1).

Rotate your wrist as you work (step 2).

Finish by pulling off the blade's tip (step 3).

Method Two for Steeling

1. Hold the steel in a near-vertical position with the tip resting on a nonslippery surface. Start with the heel of the knife against one side of the steel. Here, the chef begins with the knife touching the outer surface of the steel.

2. Maintain light pressure and use your shoulder and elbow, not your wrist, to draw the knife down the shaft of the steel in a smooth motion. Keep the steel standing straight up and down.

3. Finish the first pass by drawing the blade all the way along the shaft up to and including the tip. Repeat the entire action, this time with the blade against the steel's other side.

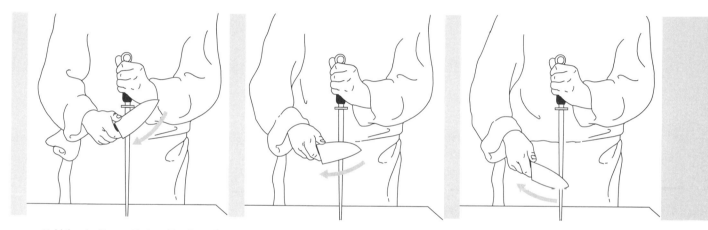

Hold the steel in a vertical position (step 1).   Use a smooth motion (step 2).   Finish the first pass (step 3).

Keeping Knives Clean and Sanitized

Keeping your knives clean helps to extend their lives. Clean knives in hot, soapy water and dry thoroughly between cutting tasks and after use and before storage. Sanitize them by wiping down the blade and handle with a sanitizing solution as necessary so that the tool does not become a site for food cross contamination.

Do not clean knives in a dishwasher—wooden handles are likely to warp and split and edges could be damaged by jostling or temperature extremes.

Never drop a knife into a pot sink. The blade could be dented or nicked by heavy pots, and someone who reaches into the sink could be seriously cut.

Storing Knives

There are a number of safe, practical ways to store knives: in knife kits or cases for one's personal collection, and wall- or tabletop-mounted racks. Proper storage prevents damage to the blade and harm to unwary individuals.

When knives are stored loosely, as in many knife kits and often in drawers, plastic knife guards or handmade sheaths can add an extra level of protection.

Designed for the professional chef, a portable case is a safe, convenient home for a large collection of knives and other kitchen utensils. Each knife fits into a particular slot so there is little risk of clanking about. A case made of vinyl can be easily cleaned and sanitized—cloth and leather cases (or rolls) cannot be cleaned as easily.

Steel- and rubber-slotted holders are more sanitary and easier to keep clean than wood-slotted holders or blocks. The steel is not porous like wood and cannot harbor microorganisms; the rubber is removable and may be washed and sanitized—even in the dishwasher.

Slotted hangers should always be mounted on the wall, not on the side of a table, as the exposed blade can present a safety hazard.

Traveling with Knives

It is sometimes necessary for professional cooks and chefs to travel by air. The fear of losing your knives or having them damaged due to mishandling might make you reluctant to check your knives as regular baggage, but airline safety regulations do not allow them as standard carry-on luggage. Be sure to pack them carefully, with sheaths covering the blades, in a case that keeps them from shifting around during handling. If you are worried that your knives may not make it to your destination with you, call ahead to arrange for a backup kit to be on hand.

Other options for storing knives in the kitchen include custom-built drawer systems, slotted to hold the blade securely in place, and magnetized bars, which can be mounted on a wall.

Setting Up Your Work Area

When you set up your work area properly, your work gets easier. The perfect setup depends upon your height, whether you are right- or left-handed, the type of work you are doing, and the surfaces (and surface area) you have available.

Preventing Stress and Fatigue

Chefs and cooks spend a lot of time on their feet, doing repetitive tasks like chopping or whisking. Good posture and general fitness help avoid back strain and fatigue as you work. Regular exercise can improve your posture and fitness as well as strength, flexibility, stamina, and even your ability to concentrate. Sturdy, supportive shoes are a must, as are good-quality socks that cushion and protect your feet.

Repetitive stress injuries are common in the kitchen. Instead of doing the same task for a long stretch, try to break up tasks into smaller segments or shorter sequences.

The stresses on your body can be counterbalanced if you take the time to create a logical work flow and to organize your tools and ingredients. The direction of the flow of work depends upon whether you are left- or right-handed. A right-handed chef arranges the work so that if moves from right to left. Reverse the flow if you are left-handed. The basic rule is to keep all products moving in one direction. You may need to change your stance from time to time, but avoid twisting the trunk of your body in the opposite direction from your legs.

Cutting Surfaces

Wooden or composition cutting boards should always be used when cutting foods. Today, many kitchens use color-coded boards to help prevent cross contamination. Be sure to observe the guidelines of your kitchen. Cutting directly on metal, glass, or marble surfaces will dull and eventually damage the blade of a knife.

Select a cutting board of the appropriate size and check to be sure it is not seriously gouged or chipped. Cutting boards should be flat, with a smooth surface. If they become deeply gouged or chipped, they should be either resurfaced or replaced. It is difficult and dangerous to work on a warped cutting board because it cannot be kept stable.

Your work surface should be a height that doesn't force you to either stoop or reach up at an uncomfortable angle. It should be stable and secure. To keep the board from slipping or rocking as you work, set it on a clean dampened side towel or a rubber mat.

Keeping Food Contact Surfaces Safe

Since most food-borne illnesses are caused by unsafe food-handling techniques, be sure to set up your work station in a way that makes safe food-handling practices second nature. Cross contamination of foods occurs when a contaminated item—for example, an egg shell with salmonella—comes in contact with another surface such as your knife, cutting board, towel, hands, or gloves. Your work station mise en place must include a container of sanitizing solution, clean wiping clothes, side towels, and disposable food-handling gloves.

Be sure to wipe down the board frequently as you work to remove peels, trim, and other debris. When you switch from one type of food to another (from chicken to cabbage, for instance), remember to sanitize the board. Use a clean towel or cleaning cloth that has been wrung out in sanitizing solution. To prevent your sanitizing solution from becoming dirty too quickly, be sure to wipe down the board with a damp, clean cloth before swabbing with the sanitizing solution.

Clean cutting boards carefully after you are finished working on them. Boards should be scrubbed in hot, soapy water, rinsed thoroughly, and then submerged in a sanitizing solution for the appropriate amount of time. Once they have drained, cutting boards should be stored in such a way that air can circulate around all surfaces so they will dry thoroughly.

If the cutting surface you use is a large tabletop board, first wipe down the entire board. Bring a container of clean, soapy water to the board and use a scrub brush or scrubbing pad to clean the entire surface carefully. Scrape away the soapy water and any residue that is lifted with a bench scraper. Wipe down the board carefully with a clean, damp cloth to remove any traces of soap. Finally, wipe down the entire surface with a clean cloth that has been wrung out in a sanitizing solution.

Keeping Foods Safe

Keep the foods you are working with safe through every step of preparation. Keep perishable and potentially hazardous foods well chilled to avoid food-borne illnesses. This may mean setting up ice baths to hold foods as you work if your work area doesn't have easy access to refrigeration. Some foods, however, are safe at room temperature and may also be easier to cut at room temperature. But if you have any doubt about the potential danger of holding any food at room temperature, it is better to err on the side of safety and keep things cold.

Have on hand enough containers to hold (separately) each of the following: prepped items ready to use in other preparations or to serve as is; wholesome trim to use in preparations such as stocks or soups; and inedible trim and other refuse. Be sure to have a separate container for composting if your kitchen is equipped to compost food scraps.

If part of your prep work includes portioning raw materials, have a scale or other portioning equipment ready, making sure that it is properly cleaned before you begin work. Cover the food-contact surface of the scale with plastic wrap, parchment paper, butcher's paper, or deli paper. This makes later cleanup easier, of course, and helps prevent cross contamination. Change the wrap between each type of product as well.

Food-Handling Gloves

Since 1992, New York State law requires all food handlers to wear food-handling gloves whenever they touch foods that will not be cooked to a safe service temperature before they are served to the customer. Other states have similar requirements, and a number of food-service operations have also made the use of gloves mandatory. Gloves must be used properly if they are to keep the food safe from cross contamination.

Remember that your gloves are not a magic barrier to pathogens, and they do not take the place of thorough and proper hand washing. Gloves themselves can become contaminated. Do not switch from one food type to another (for example, from sliced turkey to fruit salad) without changing your gloves. If a glove tears or rips, replace it right away. Replace your gloves whenever you have left your station, for any reason.

Your gloves should fit close to your hand. Gloves that are too large may slip as you work. Gloves that are too small will not only be uncomfortable, they will tear easily.

Holding the Knife

Your ability to control the knife as you work is an important factor in working safely and efficiently. The way you hold the knife can change the way you work. For instance, when you need to exert of lot of pressure, you'll want to hold the knife in a firm grip. Otherwise, the knife could simply glance off whatever it is you are cutting; it might even fly out of your hand. When you need to maneuver the knife blade around delicate fish bones, you hold the knife so that it is more like an extension of your fingers. Basic knife grips are described below, along with basic positions for your guiding hand. The guiding hand controls the food you are cutting. The position for your guiding hand depends upon the cutting technique you are using as well as the food.

Keep the fingers of the guiding hand tucked under.

Basic Knife Grips

Your choice of knife grip depends on the particular task and the specific knife. The four basic grips are as follows:

» **Grip the handle with four fingers and hold the thumb firmly against the blade's spine.**

» **Grip the handle with all four fingers and hold the thumb gently but firmly against the side of the blade.**

» **Grip the handle with three fingers, rest the index finger flat against the blade on one side, and hold the thumb on the opposite side to give additional stability and control.**

» **Grip the handle overhand, with the knife held vertically. This grip is used with a boning knife for meat fabrication tasks.**

The Guiding Hand

The guiding hand is responsible for controlling the food you are cutting. Just as your knife grip is determined by your personal preference and the cutting task at hand, so is the position of your guiding hand.

One classic position for the guiding hand calls for your fingertips to be tucked under slightly. Hold the object with the thumb held back from the fingertips. The knife blade then rests against your knuckles, preventing you from cutting your fingers.

When you peel or trim foods, cut them into tournés, or flute them, you may find yourself holding the food in the air, above the cutting surface. In that case, the guiding hand holds and turns the food against the blade to make the work more efficient. Be sure that the food, your hands, and the knife handle are all very dry.

Certain cutting techniques, such as butterflying meats or slicing a bagel in half, call for the guiding hand to be placed on top of the food to keep it from slipping while the cut is made into the food parallel or at an angle to the work surface. Holding your hand flat on the upper surface of the food with a little pressure makes these cuts safe to perform.

The guiding hand is also used to hold a carving or kitchen fork when disjointing or carving cooked meats and poultry in front of customers. The tines of the fork can be laid flat on the surface of the food or inserted directly into the item to hold it in place as it is carved.

Trimming, Peeling, and Squaring Off

Some foods require some preliminary trimming, peeling, or squaring off to remove the inedible portions or make subsequent cuts easier to perform.

Trimming tasks include removing root and stem ends from fruits, herbs, and vegetables.

Peeling tasks can be done using a rotary peeler if the skin is not too thick; carrot, potato, and similar skins are easy to remove with a peeler. Remember that these peelers work in both directions.

Removing cantaloupe rind.

Paring knives are used to trim many vegetables and fruits by cutting a thin layer away from the exterior of the food.

A chef's knife is required for vegetables, fruits, and other foods with thick rinds or skins, such as hard-skinned melons, squashes, and pineapples.

Exterior fat, gristle, and sinew can be removed from meats and poultry with a boning knife.

Foods that are naturally round can be difficult to control as you cut them. A slice can be removed from the bottom or side of a round food to make it sit flat on the cutting board, as was done to make peeling this melon easier.

Squaring off is done by cutting away slices from the top and bottom and both sides and ends of round vegetables, such as potatoes and turnips, to give them more regular dimensions, important whenever you are doing precision cutting tasks, such as cutting julienne or dicing (see pages 65–68). Slices can be cut from the ends and top of the vegetable to create a rectangle or square.

Chopping and Mincing Foods

To chop food, you cut it into pieces that are roughly the same size, but it is not critical to cut them to the exact dimensions called for when you dice or julienne an item. Mirepoix is generally chopped, as are mushrooms for duxelles, and other aromatic vegetables, fruits, or herbs that you will eventually strain out of the item you are preparing. It is also appropriate for foods you intend to purée.

Although the term "chopping" is sometimes used interchangeably with "mincing," there is a distinction. Minced foods are generally cut into a finer size. The technique shown on page 58 for mincing a shallot is essentially the same as the technique used to dice or mince an onion (page 77). Scallions and herbs are minced in a slightly different fashion. Rather than cutting repeatedly through scallions or chives, they are sliced very fine.

Mincing a Shallot

1. Trim the root and stem ends and peel the item if necessary. Since shallots (like onions and leeks) grow in layers, you can leave a bit of the root end intact to hold the layers together as you work. For other ingredients, trim and peel away the entire root and stem ends, as well as heavy or inedible skins. Make parallel cuts through the food in one direction—the more closely spaced these cuts, the smaller and finer the finished cut will be. For shallots and onions, be sure that the cuts are up to—but not completely through—the intact root end.

2. Make a horizontal cut through the layers as shown for shallots and onions. For other foods, you may simply stack up the slices you cut in step 1 and turn them so that your new slices cut them into sticks. Keep the spacing between these cuts consistent for a more nearly uniform cut.

3. Finally, cut or slice through the layers, cutting across the previous cuts you have made. This produces small pieces, shaped like cubes. The difference between chopping and mincing and dicing (see page xxx) comes down to the uniformity and precision of your cuts. Chopping and mincing need not produce a perfectly neat cut, but all the pieces should be roughly the same size.

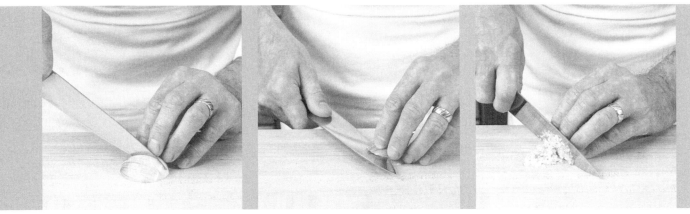

Make closely spaced vertical cuts (step 1).   Make a horizontal cut (step 2).   Cut across the grain to mince or chop (step 3).

Shredding and Grating

Shredded or grated items can be coarse or fine, depending upon the intended use. You can cut foods into a fine shred with a knife, as described on page xxx. You can also use a variety of special shredding and grating equipment including electric slicers, the shredding tools and attachments available for food processors, stand mixers, and food choppers, as well as mandolines or box graters.

When cutting tight heads of greens, such as Belgian endive and head cabbage, cut the head into halves, quarters, or smaller wedges and remove the core before cutting shreds with a chef's knife. The tip of the knife either remains in contact with the board as you cut or comes in contact with the board as you make a smooth downward slicing stroke. The blade's edge rocks onto and off of the cutting surface with each stroke.

Using a Rasp

A rasp, also referred to as a microplane, has sharp teeth that can scrape the surface of foods such as hard cheeses, spices, and citrus zest into fine shavings. Rasps can produce specific effects, depending on the size of the openings on their flat sides. Rasps come in several sizes, from a very fine and small version used for nutmeg to large rasps with larger openings to grate cheeses.

Zesting lemon with a microplane.

Using a Ginger Grater

A ginger grater is a special type of grating tool designed to release as much flavor as possible from gingerroot. Peel the gingerroot using a spoon to remove a thin layer without cutting away too much flesh. Then, scrape the peeled ginger over the grater. Use a small dish to collect the ginger and the juices released by the grater.

Grating peeled ginger with a grater.

Slicing Cuts: Plain and Decorative

When a knife is properly sharpened, it slices cleanly through food, making your work easier, even effortless. Simply guide the knife through the food, keeping the cut straight and even and letting the knife do the work.

The length of your stroke and the pressure you exert on the food should be adjusted to suit the texture of the food you are slicing. To make a long, smooth stroke, use a knife with a long blade. A salmon slicer is long and thin enough to produce very thin slices without sawing the blade back and forth.

To cut through a pâté en croûte, you may need to use a serrated knife for the crust. Because the pastry is delicate and could shatter, you need to make short back-and-forth cuts until you cut through the crust. Once the top crust has been cut, you may wish to use the index and middle fingers of your guiding hand to hold the slice as you continue to cut. Your strokes should increase in length, and you can exert a little more force on the downward stroke to cut through the pâté.

Galantines and other garnished or filled items need to be sliced carefully to keep the arrangement of the dish intact. Dip your knife into a container of warm water to make it easier to cut cleanly with the least amount of pressure.

If you can make clean, even slices, you can fabricate boneless cuts of meat into steaks or medallions or boneless fish fillets into portions; and carve roasted meats (see pages 103–119).

The following pages describe how to cut fruits, vegetables, and herbs in a variety of ways including chiffonade (very thin slices or shreds of leafy foods), rondelles (or rounds), ribbons, diagonal cuts, ripple cuts, and oblique (roll) cuts.

Chiffonade

The chiffonade cut is done by hand to cut herbs, leafy greens, and other ingredients into very fine shreds. Chiffonade is distinct from shredding, however, in that the cuts are much finer and uniform.

Basil Chiffonade

1. **For greens with large, loose leaves, such as basil, spinach, or lettuce, roll individual leaves into tight cylinders before cutting. Stack several smaller leaves before cutting.**

2. **Use a chef's knife to make the very fine, parallel cuts necessary to produce fine shreds.**

Cutting basil chiffonade.

Rondelles or Rounds

Rondelles, or rounds, are simple to cut. The shape is the result of cutting a cylindrical vegetable, such as a carrot, crosswise.

1. **Trim and peel the vegetable as necessary.**

2. **Make parallel slicing cuts through the vegetable at even intervals using a chef's knife, slicer, utility knife, electric slicer, or mandoline. The basic rondelle shape, a round disk, can be varied by cutting the vegetable on the diagonal to produce an elongated or oval disk, or by slicing the vegetable in half for half-moons. If the vegetable is scored with a channel knife before slicing, a flower is produced.**

The blade is perpendicular to the food for rondelles.

Diagonal

The diagonal cut is often used to prepare vegetables for stir-fries and other Asian-style dishes. Because it exposes a greater surface area of the vegetable, this cut shortens cooking time.

1. **Place the peeled or trimmed vegetable on the work surface.**

2. **Make a series of even, parallel cuts of the desired thickness, holding the knife so that the cuts are made at an angle, rather than making a perpendicular cross cut.**

Oblique or Roll Cut

Oblique, as it refers to a vegetable cut, reflects the fact that the cut sides are neither parallel (side by side) nor perpendicular (at right angles). This effect is achieved by rolling the vegetable a half-turn after each cut. This cut is used for long, cylindrical vegetables, such as parsnips, carrots, and celery. There are no specific dimensions for the oblique cut; the angle at which the cuts are made should be closed or opened, as required, to produce pieces of approximately the same size.

1. **Place the peeled vegetable on a cutting board. Make a diagonal cut to remove the stem end.**

2. **Hold the knife in the same position and roll the vegetable 180 degrees (a half-turn). Slice through it on the same diagonal, forming a piece with two angled edges.**

3. **Repeat until the entire vegetable has been cut.**

The blade is at an angle to the food for the roll cut.

Precision and Portioning Cuts

Precision cuts are used when nearly perfect uniformity is required. The ability to produce neat, even cuts shows your skill and craftsmanship, of course. More importantly, it means that foods cook evenly and retain the best possible flavor, nutrition, color, and appearance as they cook.

Portioning cuts are important when fabricating steaks, scallops, chops, fillets, and other portions of meat, fish, and poultry. Keeping the cuts of a consistent size and shape is important both to keep your customer happy and to keep your food costs low. These cuts are described on pages 99–119.

The dimensions included in the instructions on the following pages are considered standards. However, they can and should be adjusted to suit the type of work you are doing—à la carte versus large-volume banquet work, for example. In other words, you may hand-cut foods for small-volume work to exact specifications, while for a banquet, it is more reasonable to use equipment such as slicers, choppers, and other machines to produce reasonably similar sizes.

Another factor to keep in mind when making precision cuts is the way you will serve the food. Even though the standard julienne cut is understood to be ⅛ inch square and 1 to 2 inches long, you should adjust the cut as necessary to make foods both attractive and easy to eat; for example, batonnet and julienne should not be so long that they fall off the spoon or fork when you eat them.

Classic Names for Potato Cuts

A few special cuts associated with potatoes are produced using the same techniques as for julienne:

Pommes pailles ("straw" potatoes) are an extremely fine julienne (less than ¹⁄₁₆ inch square) cut to the desired length. Straw potatoes can also be cut into thin slices using a mandoline. Set the mandoline to a very narrow opening. Cut the slices into pailles by hand.

Pommes allumettes ("matchstick" potatoes) are cut to the same dimensions as a fine julienne.

Pommes pont neuf got their name for their resemblance to a famous bridge in Paris known as the Pont Neuf, or the "new bridge." A common English equivalent name is "steak fries." The potatoes are cut so that the rounded edge of the potato is not trimmed away, thus producing the bridge shape. When executed as a precision cut, the potatoes are trimmed so the pieces have straight sides.

Julienne and Bâtonnet

Julienne and bâtonnet are long, rectangular cuts. Related cuts are the standard pommes frites and pommes pont neuf cuts (both are names for french fries) and the allumette or "matchstick" cut. The size of the final product makes the difference in the name of each cut.

» **Fine julienne cuts are ¹⁄₁₆ inch by ¹⁄₁₆ inch thick and 1 to 2 inches long.**

» **Julienne (or allumette) cuts are ⅛ inch by ⅛ inch thick and 1 to 2 inches long.**

» **Bâtonnet cuts are ¼ inch by ¼ inch thick and 2 to 2½ inches long.**

These dimensions may be modified slightly to suit a specific need. The key point to keep in mind is that each cut should be nearly identical in dimension to all others for even cooking and the best appearance.

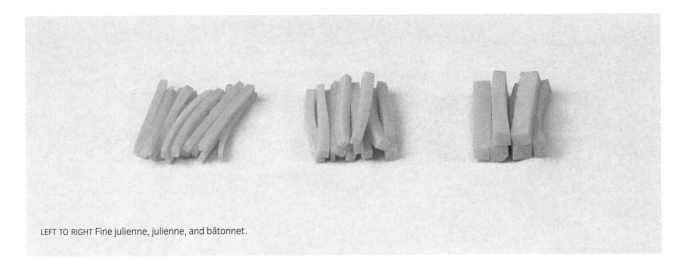

LEFT TO RIGHT Fine julienne, julienne, and bâtonnet.

1. **Trim the vegetable so that the sides are straight, which makes it easier to produce even cuts. The trimmings can be used, as appropriate, for stocks, soups, purées, or any preparation where shape is not important.**

2. **Slice the vegetable lengthwise, using parallel cuts of the proper thickness.**

3. **Stack the slices, aligning the edges, and make parallel cuts of the same thickness through the stack.**

Dice

Dicing is a cutting technique that produces cubes. To prepare vegetables for dice, first trim and peel as needed. If very precise cuts that are consistent in shape and size are the goal, cut slices away from the sides and ends of trimmed and peeled vegetables to square off the vegetable and create perfectly straight sides. Use the uneven slices you trimmed away in soups, stews, purées, or stocks whenever appropriate.

Cut the vegetable into slices of the appropriate thickness. The first cuts determine the size of the finished cut. To make a large dice or cube, space the cuts ¾ inch apart (or more, for large cubes). The smallest dice is known as brunoise. The name derives from the French verb *brunoir* ("to brown"), and reflects the common practice of sautéing these finely diced vegetables. To make larger dice, cut the slices to the thickness that you wish the finished dice to be.

» **Large dice (or cube) is a ¾-inch cube.**

» **Medium dice measures ½ inch.**

» **Small dice (cut from a bâtonnet) measures ¼ inch.**

» **Brunoise (cut from julienne) measures ⅛ inch.**

» **Fine brunoise (cut from fine julienne) measures ¹⁄₁₆ inch.**

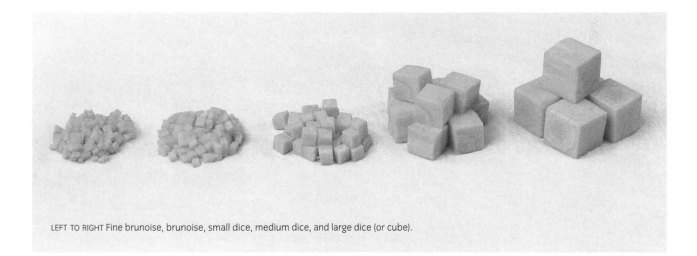

LEFT TO RIGHT Fine brunoise, brunoise, small dice, medium dice, and large dice (or cube).

Cutting Dice

1. Peel and trim the vegetable according to type. If you want very precise cuts, cut slices away from the sides and ends to produce a rectangle or square. Cut the vegetable into slices of the appropriate thickness. The first cuts determine the size of the finished cut. To make a large dice or cube, space the cuts ¾ inch apart (or more, for large cubes), and for fine brunoise, make them ¹⁄₁₆ inch apart.

2. Stack the slices on top of one another and cut through the stack. The cuts should be parallel to each other and should be the same distance apart as your initial cuts. Be sure not to stack too high; otherwise, the slices slide as you cut, producing uneven cuts.

3. Gather the sticks together; use your guiding hand to hold them in place and make crosswise parallel cuts through the sticks. These cuts should be spaced the same distance apart as the initial slices to produce perfectly even, neat dice.

Cut even slices of a consistent thickness (step 1).   Cut the slices into sticks (step 2).   Cut the sticks into dice (step 3).

Decorative and Special Cutting Techniques

These cuts are used for garnish items or to improve the appearance of a finished dish, and to give your plates or platters a special look. They typically generate a significant amount of trim. The trim from these items can be put to good use, if you are careful to properly rinse and clean the vegetable. You may peel some items before cutting them into tournés or preparing parisienne-style cuts; the trim then can be used to make purées and coulis. (For more information on these preparations, refer to *The Professional Chef, 8th Edition*.)

Paysanne and Fermière

Cuts in the paysanne ("peasant") or fermière ("farmer") styles are generally used in dishes intended to have a home-style appeal. When used for traditional regional specialties, you may opt to cut them in such a way that the shape of the vegetable's natural curves or uneven edges still show in the finished cut. However, it is important that the vegetables are cut to the same thickness so that they will cook properly and evenly.

For a more rustic presentation, cut the vegetable into halves, quarters, or eighths, depending on its size. The pieces should be roughly similar in dimension to a bâtonnet (¼ inch by ¼ inch thick and 2 to 2½ inches long). Then make even, thin crosswise cuts at roughly ⅛-inch intervals to make paysanne or fermière cuts.

When paysanne or fermière cuts are used as an ingredient in a classical dish or for a more upscale setting, cut the vegetables more precisely: Square off the vegetable first and make ½-inch-thick bâtonnet; cut the bâtonnet crosswise at ⅛-inch intervals.

Lozenge

The lozenge, or diamond, cut is most often used to prepare a vegetable garnish. To make this cut, make thin slices (generally about ¼ inch thick). Cut the slices into strips about ½ inch wide. Holding the knife at an angle to the strip, make parallel cuts that produce a diamond shape.

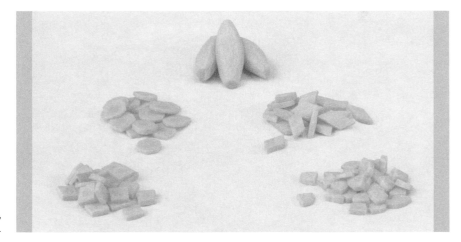

CLOCKWISE FROM BOTTOM LEFT Paysannes, rondelles, tournés, fermières, and lozenges.

Tourné

Turning (*tourner,* in French) vegetables requires a series of cuts that simultaneously trim and shape the vegetable. The shape may be similar to a barrel or a football. This is often regarded as one of the most demanding, time-consuming, and exacting cuts.

To produce classic tournés, you should cut the vegetable so that it has seven sides or faces. The faces should be smooth, evenly spaced, and tapered so that both ends are narrower than the center. A form of tournéing that removes the seeds or core from a vegetable can be used with zucchini, cucumbers, and carrots. These tournés generally have four or fewer sides. Make certain that, whichever tourné style you use, all the pieces are cut uniformly.

1. Peel the vegetable, if desired or necessary. If the trimmings can be used with the peel still intact, or if there is no appropriate use for the trimmings, you do not need to peel the vegetable.

2. Cut the vegetable into pieces of manageable size. Cut large round or oval vegetables such as beets and potatoes into quarters, sixths, or eighths (depending on their size), so the pieces are slightly longer than 2 inches. Cut cylindrical vegetables such as carrots into 2-inch pieces. To make tournés with flat bottoms and three to four faces, cut the vegetable, such as zucchini, in half lengthwise before cutting it into sections.

3. Hold the vegetable in your guiding hand. Using a paring knife or tourné knife, carve the pieces into barrel or football shapes.

Tournéing a turnip (step 3).

Fluting

This technique takes some practice to master, but the result makes an attractive garnish. It is customarily used on firm, white mushrooms. Some chefs like to pull off the tender skin covering the cap to make a *very* white mushroom.

To keep the mushroom clean while working with it, cut away the portion of the stem that was growing underground. Leave the remaining mushroom stem intact to flute the cap to make it easier to control the mushroom and prevent the cap from falling apart or breaking as it is cut.

Fluting a Mushroom

1. Hold the mushroom between the thumb and forefinger of the guiding hand. Place the blade of a paring knife or a tourné knife at an angle against the center of the mushroom cap. Rest the thumb of the cutting hand on the mushroom and use it to brace the knife.

2. Rotate the knife toward the cap edge to cut a shallow groove. At the same time the knife blade is cutting, use the guiding hand to turn the mushroom in the opposite direction. (Some chefs like to hold the knife with the blade pointing toward them and make cuts that start at the top of the cap and end at the edge. Others prefer to hold the knife with the blade pointing away from them and make the cuts in the opposite direction, starting at the edge of the cap and finishing at the top.)

3. Turn the mushroom slightly and repeat the cutting steps. Continue until the entire cap is fluted. Pull the trimmings away. Trim away the stem after the cap is fluted. Finish the cap by pressing a design such as a star or a fish into the center of the cap with the tip of the paring knife.

The start of a stroke (step 1).   The middle of a stroke (step 2).   The stroke is complete (step 3).

Parisiennes

A parisienne scoop (or a melon baller) is used to make uniform balls of fruits or vegetables. This can create a significant amount of trim loss. The technique described here produces the neatest scoops with the least possible loss.

1. **Trim or peel the vegetable or fruit so that the solid flesh is exposed. Twist the scoop into the flesh, pushing down to fully recess it. This produces a round ball without a flat side.**

2. **Work to an even depth over the surface of the vegetable or fruit. Once all the scoops possible have been removed from the top portion, slice away the scooped part to create a fresh layer that can be scooped again. If the vegetable or fruit might discolor as you work, hold it in cold water.**

Making parisienne potatoes.

Gaufrettes

Gaufrette means "waffle" in French—a good description of this special cut.

You need a mandoline to make a gaufrette cut. You can cut a variety of vegetables and fruits this way. It is most commonly used with solid foods that have a dense and uniform texture: potatoes, sweet potatoes, carrots, zucchini, or yellow squash. If the vegetable you are cutting might discolor after you slice it, hold the slices in a container of cold water to prevent exposure to the air. If necessary, add a little lemon juice or vinegar to keeps foods from turning brown.

Potato Gaufrettes

1. Set the mandoline blades so that the slicing blade and the julienne teeth are both opened to the appropriate thickness.

2. Make the first pass, running the vegetable the entire length of the mandoline. This scores the vegetable, but does not cut a slice completely away.

3. Turn the vegetable 90 degrees and repeat the entire stroke. This second pass over the blades creates an open, waffle texture. It also cuts the slice completely away from the vegetable. Continue to cut the vegetable, turning it 90 degrees each time you complete a pass.

Making gaufrette slices on a mandoline.

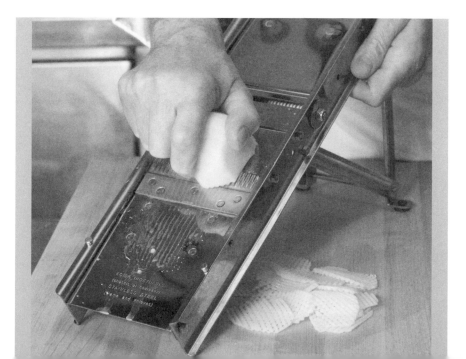

3

CUTTING TECHNIQUES FOR VEGETABLES AND FRUITS

Different foods have different characteristics.

The cutting techniques described in the previous chapter must be modified somewhat so that you can cut foods that may have unusual shapes or textures.

Learning the way to handle individual fruits and vegetables means knowing how to remove peels, seeds, stems, and roots, in some cases. In others, you need to have a strategy to keep foods such as potatoes and apples from turning brown as you work. Leeks illustrate the need to thoroughly wash fresh produce; layers and rough surfaces tend to trap dirt.

Once trimmed, some fruits and vegetables are simple to cut. Potatoes, carrots, celery, and turnips, for instance, have a relatively uniform texture. These foods can be cut into slices, sticks, dice, or other cuts described in Chapter 2, pages 61–73.

Foods that grow in layers (leeks, onions, fennel, and shallots, for instance) all require special handling in order to produce even-size cuts. Apples, peppers, and mangos are examples of ingredients with seeds, cores, or pits that you must work around. Knowing the right technique for a specific vegetable or fruit means that you can minimize trim loss.

Vegetables

The right vegetable cut makes all the difference in soups, sauces, side dishes, salads, and garnishes. The more uniform and precise the cut, the better the appearance and flavor of the dish. Cooking times are more uniform, so you are less likely to end up with an unevenly cooked dish. The techniques in this section include techniques for vegetables to use as aromatics, such as garlic or leeks, as well as mushrooms and tomatoes.

Onions

There are many different ways to cut an onion. Some methods have the advantage of speed, important in volume cooking situations. Others produce very little waste, appropriate when there is no use for the trim. Still others are best when precise, even cuts are required. Select a method based on your specific needs.

Onions can bring tears to your eyes. Although there are many home-style remedies, the best advice is to use a very sharp knife so that the onion will be cut, not crushed.

To streamline your prep work, you can peel onions the day before you cut and cook them. Onions to be served raw should be cut at the last possible moment. As onions sit, they lose their flavor and develop a strong, unpleasant odor in a short time. If a portion of your sliced raw onions remains unused at the end of a shift, it should be added to a mirepoix, included in a stock or broth as it simmers, or, if there are no other uses, put in the compost bucket or thrown out.

Peeling and Cutting an Onion

1. Use a paring knife to remove the stem end of the onion. Peel off the skin and the underlying layer, if it contains brown spots. Trim the root end but leave it intact. Halve the onion lengthwise through the root. Put it cut side down on a cutting board and make a series of evenly spaced, parallel, lengthwise cuts with the tip of a chef's knife, again leaving the root end intact.

2. Make two or three horizontal cuts in the onion (parallel to the board) from the stem end toward the root end (do not cut all the way through) while gently holding the vertical cuts together. Holding the previous cuts together will help to produce a more uniform mince.

3. Make even crosswise cuts with a chef's knife all the way through from stem to root end. The closer the cuts in step 1 and in this step, the finer the dice will be. An alternative method for slicing or dicing an onion calls for a series of cuts to be made following the natural curve of the onion half (this approach eliminates the need to make a horizontal cut, as directed in step 2). Make a series of cuts evenly spaced over the curved surface of the onion (sometimes referred to as radial cuts) and then make crosswise cuts for dice or mince.

Make parallel cuts (step 1).   Make even horizontal cuts (step 2).   Cut the onion crosswise to dice (step 3).

Cutting Onions into Julienne, Slices, and Rings To cut onions into julienne, trim, peel, and halve the onion as directed above for making dice. Cut out the stem end by making a cut around the stem to create a notch so that the slices will separate into individual julienne after making a series of lengthwise cuts evenly spaced over the curved surface of the onion.

To slice an onion for sandwiches, trim and peel the onion. Use a slicer, a mandoline, or a chef's knife to cut across the onion up to the stem end. You will find it easiest to control the onion as you work if you leave the stem intact. Thicker slices, such as you might make for grilled onions, may fall apart. If you want them to stay intact, hold the layers together with toothpicks or skewers.

To make onion rings, cut the onion crosswise into slices and then pull the layers apart. Onion rings can be included in salads, used as a garnish, or dipped in batter or breading to deep-fry.

Shallots

Shallots are like onions in that they grow in layers. They also are like garlic in that they grow in cloves. To mince shallots, first trim and peel the shallots as you would an onion.

If the shallot has more than one clove, separate the cloves and make a series of perpendicular and horizontal cuts using the tip of your chef's knife, or a paring knife. (Mincing a shallot is shown on page 58.)

Scallions

To remove wilted outer layers from scallions, ramps, or small leeks, catch the layer you wish to remove between your thumb and the flat of a knife blade and pull the layer away. The next step, before slicing or mincing, is to trim away the root end.

By opening or closing the angle of your cut, you can cut the green tops of scallions on the diagonal. Slice through the scallion to create thin rounds. Chop or mince the light-green and white parts to use as a finishing or garnishing ingredient.

Slice scallions at an angle to produce diagonal cuts.

Garlic

Chefs know that all members of the onion family have the best flavor and texture when you cut them by hand just before you cook them. Preparing garlic and shallots is part of the kitchen's daily mise en place. Large quantities of garlic may be minced in a food processor. You may wish to add a small amount of oil to the garlic as it is being minced. If you have some uncooked minced garlic or shallots left over at the end of a shift, store them covered in oil under refrigeration for a maximum of twenty-four hours.

To separate a head of garlic into cloves, wrap it in a side towel. The towel keeps the papery skin from flying around your work area. Use the heel of your hand or a closed fist to hit the head and break it into individual cloves. Break or cut the cloves cleanly away from the root end.

To peel individual cloves, set the garlic on a work surface. Position the flat side of a chef's knife on top of the clove. Use a closed fist or the heel of your hand to hit the blade onto the clove to split the skin open and make it easy to peel it away. If you hit the garlic too firmly, though, the cloves will be crushed, so use a lighter touch if you want to leave the garlic cloves whole.

Special garlic peelers make it easy to peel the cloves; slicers can be used to shave paper-thin slices of garlic for sauces and sautés; and food processors or garlic presses are used by some to make puréed garlic. However, you can perform all these tasks with a sharp knife and a clean side towel, and have an easier cleanup and a better-quality product. Once this technique is mastered, it takes very little time to properly peel, slice, or mash garlic by hand in almost all situations except high-volume cooking, where using processors or purchasing minced garlic or shallots makes the most sense.

To make a garlic paste, chop the garlic as described below, then hold the knife nearly flat against the cutting surface angle and use the cutting edge to mash the garlic against the cutting board. Repeat this step until the garlic is mashed to a paste. You may want to add a bit of salt to the garlic as you work it into a paste. The salt acts as an abrasive to help pulverize the garlic.

Chopping Garlic

1. To loosen the skin from each clove, crush it between the knife blade's flat side and the cutting board. Peel off the skin and remove the root end and any brown spots. At some times of the year and under certain storage conditions, the garlic may begin to sprout. Split the clove in half and remove the core for the best flavor.

2. Put the skinned cloves on the work surface and use a chef's knife to slice the cloves. Since you will be continuing to chop the garlic, it is not important that these slices have an even thickness.

3. Use an up-and-down motion, repeatedly lifting and lowering the heel of the knife so the blade cuts through the garlic to chop it coarsely. Keep the tip of the knife in the same position as you work. To chop or mince garlic evenly, periodically use the flat side of the blade to gather the bits of garlic together into a pile. Push the garlic clinging to the side of the blade onto the pile and continue chopping until the garlic is evenly cut.

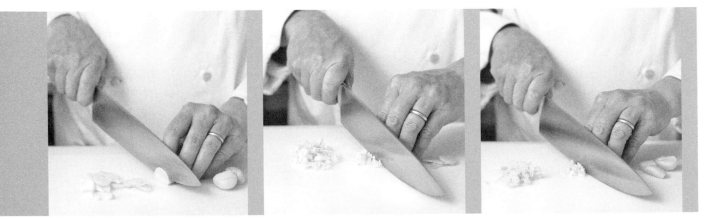

Slice peeled garlic cloves thin (step 2).   Lift the heel of your knife (step 3).   Lower the knife firmly and rapidly (step 3).

Leeks

Leeks grow in layers that are almost always filled with grit and sand. It is important to thoroughly clean leeks before cooking with them. To clean leeks, first rinse off all the surface soil, paying special attention to the roots, where dirt clings.

Cleaning Leeks

1. Put the rinsed leek on your cutting board and trim away the heavy, dark-green part of the leaves using a chef's knife. By cutting on an angle, you can avoid losing the tender light-green part of the leek. Reserve the dark-green part of the leek to make bouquet garni or for another appropriate use.

2. Trim away most of the root end, then cut the leek lengthwise into halves, thirds, or quarters.

3. Rinse the leek under running water to remove any remaining grit or sand. Now the leek can be cut into julienne or other cuts as desired.

Rinse leeks thoroughly.

Mushrooms

Clean the mushrooms just before you are ready to prepare them by rinsing quickly in cool water, just long enough to remove any dirt. Do not allow them to soak. (Some people feel that mushrooms should be cleaned by wiping with a soft cloth or brushing with a soft-bristled brush; this is not practical in a professional kitchen.) Let the mushrooms drain and dry well before slicing or mincing. The tough stems of some mushrooms, such as shiitakes, should be removed prior to slicing. White mushrooms, morels, cèpes, and portobello mushroom stems can usually be left intact, although it is a good practice to cut a slice from the stem end to trim away any dried or fibrous portions.

Mushrooms can be chopped or minced to use in preparations like duxelles or stuffings. They can also be cut into slices, julienne, bâtonnet, or dice. (The method for fluting mushrooms is shown on page 71.)

Slicing and Mincing Mushrooms

1. To slice whole mushrooms, hold the mushroom cap with your guiding hand and slice through the cap and stem, if the stem has not been trimmed off. The slices on either side of the cap will be smaller than the slices in the center. If the end slices are too small or thin, save them to flavor soups and stocks.

2. Cut the slices into julienne by cutting across the slices at the desired thickness to create a garnish for soups, sauces, or salads.

3. To mince the mushrooms for use in duxelles or other applications, turn the julienne parallel to the edge of the work surface and make crosswise cuts. These cuts need only be as neat and precise as you require for service. Garnishes should show very clean cuts, while chopped or minced mushrooms to add as an ingredient may not require as much precision.

Rest the mushroom on a "flat" side to keep it stable.

Tomatoes

Tomatoes may be peeled before they are used in cooked sauces and other dishes. To remove the peel easily, the tomatoes are dipped in boiling water to blanch them. The technique for blanching and peeling tomatoes is also suitable for peaches, apricots, and some nuts.

Once peeled, tomatoes can be seeded and then chopped, a preparation known as tomato concassé, or cut into neat dice or julienne.

Peeling and Seeding Tomatoes

1. Core the tomato, using the tip of the paring knife. Score the blossom end of the tomato to make the skin easier to remove later on, if desired (some chefs skip this step).

2. Put a few tomatoes at a time into a pot of boiling water—adding too many can lower the temperature of the water enough to slow the blanching process. After 10 to 30 seconds (depending on the tomatoes' age and ripeness), remove the tomatoes with a slotted spoon, skimmer, or spider and immediately transfer them to a container of ice water to prevent further cooking.

3. Use the tip of a paring knife to help pull away the skin. Catch the skin between the thumb and the flat side of the blade. If the tomato is ripe and was properly blanched, the skin should come away easily in a thin, translucent layer. If it does not, cut it from the tomato at the points where it adheres.

4. Cut the tomato in half. Slicing tomatoes are usually cut across the widest point (the belly), while plum (or Roma) tomatoes are cut from stem to blossom end. For chopped tomatoes, gently squeeze out the seeds. To cut the tomato for a garnish, cut it into wedges and then slice away the seeds using a paring knife, leaving behind a tomato "fillet." Cut the fillet into julienne or other shapes as desired.

Score the blossom end (step 1).   Peel away the skin (step 3).   Quarter the tomato and cut away the seeds (step 4).

Avocados

Avocados are sometimes split lengthwise in half, pitted, and filled with a stuffing with the skin still intact. For most other preparations, remove the pit and the skin, and then cut the flesh into slices, wedges, or dice. Or, simply mash avocado into a paste that is as smooth or as coarse as required.

Removing Peels and Pits from Avocados

1. To remove the skin and pit of an avocado, use the fingertips of your guiding hand to control the avocado, but don't press down too hard. Press the avocado against the knife blade to pierce the skin and cut through the flesh up to the pit. Cup the avocado gently between both hands to avoid bruising it and twist the two halves in opposite directions so they slide apart.

2. It can be difficult to remove the slippery avocado pit with your fingertips without mangling the flesh. You can "chop" the heel of a knife into the pit, then twist and pull it free from the flesh. To remove the pit from the knife safely, use the edge of the cutting board or the lip of a container to pry it free.

3. Catch the skin of the avocado between the ball of your thumb and the flat side of a blade (a utility knife is used here) and pull it free from the flesh. The avocado is ready to cut into slices, wedges, or cubes.

Twist the avocado halves in opposite directions (step 1).

Use the heel of a chef's knife to remove the pit (step 2).

Peel the avocado with a paring knife (step 3).

Fresh Peppers and Chiles

Peppers and chiles are pods with a cluster of seeds attached to the stem end and the fleshy ribs. The way you handle peppers and chiles depends upon how you intend to use them. You can cut them into rings to use as a garnish or cut them in half to fill with a stuffing. You can peel them or roast them, cook them as an ingredient in other dishes, or use them as the main ingredient in a purée.

Hot peppers (chiles) have oils that can irritate your skin. We suggest that you wear disposable gloves when working with chiles. Whether you wear gloves or not, don't touch your eyes or other sensitive areas. Wash your hands thoroughly in plenty of warm soapy water to remove any residue from your skin.

The way a fresh pepper is initially prepared determines how much of it will be lost to trim. For the least trim loss, halve the pepper lengthwise from stem to blossom end. If the pepper is large, continue to cut it into quarters. Use the tip of the paring knife to cut away the stem and the seeds. The flesh around the stem and at the blossom end of the pepper is perfectly good, although it may not be easy to cut into the exact shape needed, if appearance matters.

To prepare a pepper that you want to cut into precise julienne, bâtonnet, or dice, slice off the top and bottom of the pepper—the shoulders and the tip. Slit the pepper to open it into a rectangle, trim, and peel as shown at right. Peppers peeled this way have a fresh flavor and a crisp texture, different from peppers that are roasted before they are peeled. Peeled fresh peppers and chiles also absorb flavors from marinades and dressings better than peeled roasted peppers.

Trimming and Peeling Fresh Peppers

1. Slice the pepper crosswise through the stem and blossom ends. This removes the "shoulders" of the pepper and the pointed "tail"; the trim can be saved for other use.

2. Make a slice through the flesh on one side to open up the pepper, exposing the ribs and seeds. Hold the pepper with your guiding hand so that it is stable. Hold the knife blade parallel to the work surface and cut away the ribs and the seeds in one motion. As you work, the guiding hand unrolls the pepper, so that by the time you are done, all the seeds and ribs are cut away, and you have created a neat, relatively flat rectangle shape.

3. To cut away the skin, use your guiding hand to keep the pepper flat and stable. Insert the blade so you are cutting between the flesh and the skin.

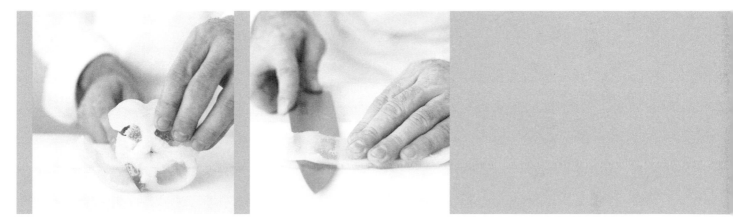

Roll the pepper away from the knife (step 2).   Cut away a thin layer to remove the peel (step 3).

Roasting Peppers Roasting peppers makes it easy to peel them. It also changes the flavor and texture of the pepper significantly. Described below are several different methods for roasting peppers.

Roasting or Broiling Peppers

1. Large quantities of peppers or chiles are often roasted in a hot oven or under a broiler, rather than charred individually in a flame. Halve the peppers or chiles and remove the stems, seeds, and ribs, if desired (the peppers or chiles can also be left whole). Place the halved peppers cut side down on an oiled sheet pan or arrange the whole peppers on their sides. Place the pan in a very hot oven or under a broiler. Roast or broil until the peppers or chiles are evenly charred.

2. Remove the pan from the oven or broiler and cover immediately with an inverted sheet pan. Let stand for 30 minutes to steam the peppers and make the skin easier to remove. Remove the stems, ribs, and seeds from the whole peppers when removing the charred skins.

Charring Peppers over an Open Flame

1. Hold a pepper or chile directly over the flame of a gas burner using tongs or a kitchen fork. (You can also char one or more peppers at a time on a hot grill). Turn the pepper as it roasts until the entire surface is evenly charred.

2. Place the peppers in a plastic or paper bag or covered bowl and let stand for at least 30 minutes to steam the skin loose.

3. Use a paring knife to remove the charred skin after it has steamed. Have a bowl of water nearby to rinse the charred skin from your knife as you work. To remove any bits of charred skin that remain on the pepper, rub lightly with a towel.

Turn the pepper as it roasts to char the skin evenly.

Fruits

Fruits are used in a variety of ways in the kitchen, from fine slivers or shreds of citrus zest to pineapple cubes and melon balls to feature in a fruit salad. Since fruits are often uncooked when they are served, be sure to observe all food safety standards, including rinsing and washing fruits carefully and wearing disposable food-handling gloves.

Zesting Citrus Fruit

Chefs use citrus juice and zest (the colored part of the peel which contains flavorful, aromatic oils) in many recipes as a final seasoning or a garnish. Cutting the fruit into wedges, slices, and suprêmes are other preparation techniques used with citrus fruit.

Citrus zest is the outer portion of a citrus fruit's peel or rind. It is used to add color, texture, aroma, and flavor to various dishes. The zest includes only the skin's brightly colored part, which contains much of the fruit's flavorful and aromatic volatile oils. It does not include the underlying white pith, which has a bitter taste.

Some chefs strongly recommend seeking out organic citrus to avoid adding pesticides and other potentially toxic residues to their dishes. Scrubbing the fruit before you zest it is a good idea, although that won't remove all unwanted substances.

If you need both zest and segments or zest and juice from a citrus fruit, cut the zest away first, using the appropriate tool (a zester is shown in the photograph at right). Work gently if you are planning to cut segments. If you press too hard on the fruit as you work, the membranes in the fruit will burst and you will lose too much juice. On the other hand, if you need juice, the action of removing the zest is as effective as rolling the fruit on a hard surface to help release more juice.

Blanch the zest before you serve it to remove any unpleasant, bitter flavors. The blanching process may also removes chemical residue from the surface. To blanch zest, cook it briefly in simmering water and then drain it in a fine sieve. Repeat as often as necessary; generally, two to three times is best.

To make candied zest, cut the zest away from the fruit in wide strips, and then cut the strips into pieces the size and shape you require. Blanch the zest as directed above. Make sugar syrup by combing 3 parts sugar with 2 parts water and simmering the syrup. Add the blanched zest to the simmering syrup and continue to simmer until the zest is translucent and tender, usually about 10 minutes. Drain the zest and roll it in fine sugar to store for later use.

If you know you need both juice and zest from the fruit, be sure to cut away the zest before you juice the fruit.

A variety of tools can be used to remove citrus zest, depending upon the effect you want.

» **Use a vegetable peeler to cut away a very thin layer of the colored portion of the skin. Once the strips are cut away, cut them into fine shreds.**

» **Use a channel knife to cut out strips. These strips can be used to garnish hot and cold drinks or prepared as candied zest.**

» **Use a citrus zester, a specialized tool that peels away long, fine, thin strips from the skin without digging deeply enough to cut away the pith.**

» **Use a microplane, rasp, or box grater to produce fine shavings. The microplane is the most efficient and produces the lightest, finest zest.**

Using a citrus zester.

Citrus Slices and Suprêmes

Citrus fruits are often sliced with the skin intact and added "as is" to fruit plates or used as a garnish. To make citrus slices easier to eat, peel them first. The peeled, segmented fruit is appreciated, but the segments are more attractive and easier to eat if they are cut away from the membrane into perfect segments—also known as "suprêmes"—after peeling.

Cutting Citrus Suprêmes

1. Cut away the blossom and stem ends of the fruit to make it easy to handle. Put the cut side of the fruit flat on the work surface and completely cut away the peel and bitter white pith of the fruit, following the natural curve of the fruit and cutting away as little flesh as possible, using the midsection of the cutting edge of a utility knife or a *yo-deba*, depending upon the size of the fruit. Turn the fruit over so the opposite flat end is resting on the board, and remove any stray bits of peel. You can cut the fruit into slices at this point, if desired.

2. Hold the fruit in your guiding hand. Work over a bowl to catch the juices as well as the suprêmes as they fall. Use a paring knife to slice between the flesh and the connective membrane on both sides of each citrus segment. Twist the knife blade very slightly as you make the cut along the second side of each segment. Use the side of the blade to push the segment completely away from the membrane and into the bowl.

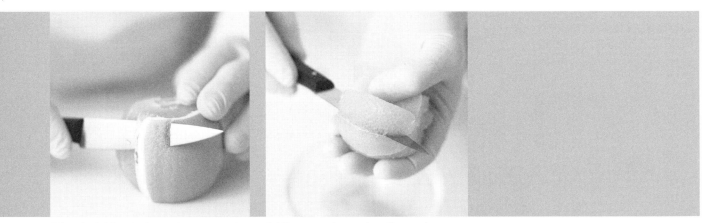

Follow the fruit's natural curve to remove peel and pith (step 1).

Cut the segments away from the membrane (step 2).

Melons

Melons can be peeled or not, depending upon the way you wish to present them. You may wish to remove the entire rind before halving the melon and removing the seeds to streamline production of fruit plates and salads. In other cases, you may prefer to leave the rind on. In that case, the melon is halved and the seeds removed.

Cut the melon as close to the time you plan to serve it as possible, because once cut, the fruit starts to "weep" and then looks dry if it sits exposed to the air for very long.

To keep the melon from rolling as you peel it, remember to cut away a thin slice from both ends. This creates a flat surface that will stay steady on the work surface.

Cutting Up a Melon

1. Use a chef's knife to cut a slice from both ends of the melon to stabilize it on the cutting surface. Cut from the top of the fruit toward the bottom using a chef's knife to cut away the rind. Use the wrist to turn the blade and follow the curve of the melon.

2. Cut the melon in half and scoop out the seeds and fiber from the center—a serving spoon is an efficient tool to scoop without gouging out too much edible flesh.

3. The melon can now be cut into slices, wedges, or balls. To make slices, transfer the halves to a cutting board and cut the fruit lengthwise to make wedges, or crosswise for slices. Wedges and slices can be cut into smaller pieces or other shapes as desired. To make melon balls, push and twist the bowl of a scoop into the flesh of the halves, working to an even depth and cutting from the outside toward the center for the most attractive cuts and the least waste.

Cut the rind away (step 1).   Scoop out the seeds carefully (step 2).   Scoop melon balls from the peeled melon (step 3).

Pineapples

To get the best yield from a pineapple, be sure to select the trimming and peeling method appropriate for the final use. The first step in any technique for cutting a pineapple calls for removing the prickly and very coarse outer skin. This can be done using one of the two methods described below. For either method, cut a slice from the base of the pineapple to steady it. Method One has the advantage of being quick. The disadvantage is that you lose a little more of the edible flesh. Method Two is attractive and gives a better yield, but it is time-consuming.

You can leave the pineapple top intact to make handling the fruit easier. The fronds also make an attractive display piece.

Once the pineapple is peeled, you can cut it into slices. To make rings, use a corer to remove the fibrous core, and then cut into slices. You can cut the pineapple lengthwise into wedges or cut the flesh into chunks of the desired size.

Method One for Peeling a Pineapple

1. Put the pineapple on its side on a cutting board. Slice off the pineapple top and a slice from the base with a chef's knife.

2. Stand the pineapple on the base and slice away the skin, following the natural curve of the sides. Make sure that the cuts are deep enough to remove the eyes, but not so deep that a great deal of edible flesh is removed.

Method Two for Peeling a Pineapple

1. Trim away the skin in the same manner as described in Method One, removing only the skin—the eyes will still be left in the flesh.

2. Once the peel is removed, the spiral pattern of the eyes is more apparent. Using a chef's knife or a utility knife, cut out the eyes by making V-shaped trenches in the flesh, following the spiral pattern.

Cut deeply enough to remove the eyes (method 1, step 1).

Slices, Cubes, Wedges, and Rings

1. To make neat dice or cubes, slice the pineapple evenly at the desired thickness until you reach the core on one side. Turn the pineapple so you can continue to make slices on all sides of the core. Cut the pineapple slices into neat julienne or bâtonnet, or dice to the appropriate size.

2. To prepare wedges or chunks, cut the peeled pineapple lengthwise into halves, quarters, or eighths, depending upon the pineapple's size or your specific needs. Cut out the core. Slice the pineapple wedges crosswise into chunks, if desired.

3. To prepare pineapple rings, slice a peeled pineapple crosswise and use a round cutter to remove the core from each slice. Or, use a large cutter, similar to an apple corer, to remove the core from the entire pineapple before cutting it crosswise into rings.

Mangos

Mangos present a unique cutting challenge because they have one wide, flat pit in the center of the flesh. The flesh adheres very tightly to the pit as well as to the skin. It is messy—but possible—to remove the skin first, by paring it away from the fruit with a paring knife, but the fruit is easier to handle if you cut it away from the pit before paring away the skin. Working from the stem end to the base keeps you cutting with the grain of the mango, another tip for better yield and cleaner cuts.

The hedgehog cut shown below can be used to create a striking element on a fruit plate, and it is also a good technique for dicing the flesh while it is still attached to the skin. Change the angle and length of the cuts to produce diamond-shaped pieces, cubes, or slices.

Once you have cut the mango away from the pit, you can peel the fruit to cut into slices, chop, or make into a puree. If the fruit is very ripe, scoop the flesh away from the skin with a serving spoon, removing as much of the flesh as possible. For slightly firmer fruit, use a paring knife or a peeler to trim away the skin. Once the skin is removed, you can cut it up as appropriate to feature in salsas, sauces, or fruit plates.

The Hedgehog Cut

1. Use a chef's knife to carefully slice as close to the pit as possible to remove the most flesh. Cut the mango away from the wide sides first, to make good-sized pieces. Make a cut slightly off-center, working from the stem end to the tip of the mango. Your knife should scrape against the pit. The narrow sides can also be cut away from the pit. They may not be large enough to cut into the shape you require, but the flesh is still useful for purées or to make smaller dice or cubes.

2. Score the flesh in a crosshatch pattern with the tip of your knife. This may be done on the diagonal to make diamond-shaped cubes, as shown in the accompanying photograph, or using perpendicular cuts to produce square or rectangular cubes.

3. Turn the mango half inside out to separate the cubes. Use the tip of the paring knife to cut the mango away from the skin, or present the mango "hedgehog" as part of a fruit plate or platter.

Slice close to the pit on both sides (step 1).

Score the flesh in a crosshatch pattern (step 2).

Turn the scored mango half inside out (step 3).

4

CUTTING TECHNIQUES FOR MEAT AND POULTRY

The difference between butchering and fabricating meats is subtle. In the broad view, however, butchering means cutting an entire animal into large cuts known as primal cuts. Subsequent cuts are made to fabricate the primal cuts into a variety of smaller cuts known as sub-primal or wholesale cuts.

Fabrication, although it involves the meat-cutting techniques used in the butcher shop, is essentially the fine-tuning of an item purchased from a butcher or meat purveyor to produce the menu cuts familiar to most chefs and restaurant patrons.

The meat industry has changed a great deal over time. At one time, the ability to butcher your own meats and poultry was a necessity. Today, most restaurants buy what are known as "boxed" meats. They have been trimmed and portioned to some extent at the packing house or processing plant before they are shipped either to purveyors or directly to the restuarant. Preparing your own meat and poultry menu cuts helps to keep food costs down, as long as trim loss is kept to a minimum. Even if you do buy portioned cuts, you will still want to do some amount of trimming or shaping.

You can improve your bottom line if you can use the wholesome trim from your meat and poultry fabrication efforts to produce a variety of items. Burgers, sausages, and pâtés are some examples. Poultry wings can be used to make bar food and appetizers. Use bones to prepare stocks or broths, and reduce your dependence on purchased bones and prepared bases.

Meat Fabrication Techniques

Even though meat is often purchased already prepared as a specific menu cut, it is important for any chef to execute some fundamental meat fabrication techniques, including tying a roast, cleaning and shaping cuts from the tenderloin, and cutting bone-in chops.

Tying Roasts

Tying a roast with secure knots that have the right tension is one of the simplest and most frequently required types of meat fabrication. It ensures that the roast will be evenly cooked and that it will retain its shape after roasting. Although simple, the technique is often one of the most frustrating to learn. For one thing, knot tying is not always easy. As long as the string is taut enough to give the roast a compact shape without being too tight, however, the result will be fine.

There is one trick to keep in mind that will make initial attempts easier. Leave the string very long, so that it will wrap easily around the entire diameter of the meat. Or, leave the string attached to the spool, and cut it only when the entire roast is tied. There are other methods used for tying roasts than the one shown here. If possible, learn other methods to tie different cuts of meat with ease.

Tying a Roast

1. The technique illustrated here works for either boneless or bone-in roasts. To begin, tie the end of the string around the thicker end of the meat (any knot that holds securely can be used). Pass the string around your outspread fingers and thumb with the string coming from behind the fingers, around the thumb, and then back behind itself. Twist the loop around so that the base of the loop twists back on itself.

2. Spread your hand open to enlarge the loop. Continue to enlarge the loop until it is wide enough to pass easily around the meat, completely encircling it.

3. Pull the loose end of the string until the loop is securely tightened around the meat. Continue until the entire piece of meat has been secured with loops. Turn over the piece of meat. Pass the loose end of the string through the loop, then pass it back underneath the loop. Pull the string tight and continue down the length of the meat. Once the string has been wrapped around each loop from one end to the other, turn the meat back over. Cut the loose end and tie the string securely to the first loop.

Open the loop of string by spreading the fingers (step 1).

Slide the loop of string over the roast (step 2).

Tighten the string and pull the knot tight (step 3).

Techniques for Tenderloins

The tenderloin is one of the most expensive cuts of meat, so care should be taken to leave the meat as intact as possible. Use a very sharp boning knife and pay close attention to each step.

The technique used to trim a beef tenderloin can also be used to trim veal, pork, game, and lamb tenderloins, as well as other cuts of meat with a tough, shiny membrane called silverskin. Some of these cuts are top rounds of beef and veal and loin cuts of venison and other large game.

Under the fat cover, surrounding the meat, is a tough membrane covering the smooth side of the tenderloin—the silverskin, which must be removed before cooking. If it is left in place, it shrinks when exposed to heat, causes uneven cooking, and spoils the appearance of the dish.

Once the tenderloin is cleaned of surface fat, the chain, and the silverskin, it is ready to tie into a roast or slice into various menus cuts (see at right). Once you have sliced the meat into the desired menu cut, you may wish to shape it with dampened cheesecloth to press it gently into a compact, uniform piece. This is done to encourage even and uniform cooking and to give the meat a more attractive look.

Some trim, especially the chain from a beef tenderloin, can be further cleaned of excess fat and used in a variety of preparations, such as stocks, broths, sauces, soups, and ground meat items.

Menu Cuts for Beef Tenderloin

The following terms are associated primarily with the beef tenderloin:

Chateaubriand Chateaubriand is a thick cut (weighing approximately 10 ounces, meant to serve 2 people) taken from the middle of the fillet. It is traditionally grilled and then served with a sauce and potatoes. The term refers more properly to a specific recipe than a cut from the tenderloin.

Tournedos Tournedos are cut from the thinner end of the tenderloin. They are rounder than the filet mignon cut, and are usually cut into pieces weighing 4 to 5 ounces.

Filet mignon Filet mignon is a cut from the tail section of the tenderloin that is too small to be properly termed a tournedo. The term *mignon* indicates something small or delicate—a small, delicate cut from the tenderloin. Filets mignons are generally cut into pieces weighing 5 to 6 ounces.

Cuts from the loin or tenderloin of other animals are generally referred to as follows:

Medallions Medallions are cut in the same manner as beef tournedos. The weight of the medallions will vary, depending upon the size of the loin or tenderloin fabricated.

Noisettes Noisettes are cut from the tenderloin or loin; they are generally smaller than a medallion.

Trimming and Shaping a Tenderloin

1. Lift and pull away the fat covering if the tenderloin is untrimmed. This fat pulls away easily, and the blade of the boning knife is used to steady the tenderloin as the fat cover is pulled away. Pull and cut away the strip of fat and meat known as the "chain."

2. Position the tenderloin so that the tail is to the left, if you are right-handed, or to the right, if you are left-handed. Work the tip of a boning knife under the silverskin; hold the end of the silverskin tight against the meat with your guiding hand and glide the knife blade just underneath the silverskin. Angle the blade upward slightly so that only the silverskin is cut away. Work so that your cuts travel from the tail (the narrow end) toward the head (the larger end of the tenderloin).

3. To make medallions and similar menu cuts (see the accompanying sidebar list), slice the tenderloin (or other boneless cuts of beef, veal, pork, lamb, or game) into portions of the size you require. Cut cheese-cloth in a square large enough to easily wrap the meat portion. Gather the cheesecloth together and twist to tighten it around the meat. As you twist the cloth with one hand, press down firmly on the meat with even, moderate pressure. Remove the cheesecloth once the desired shape is achieved.

Remove the chain (step 1).   Glide the blade just under the silverskin (step 2).   Shape medallions with cheesecloth (step 3).

Bone-In Portion Cuts

Chops and steaks are made from bone-in cuts such as rib and loin. A saw is necessary to cut through bones. Large bones can be difficult to saw through, but the rib and loin of pork, lamb, venison, and beef have more manageable bones.

Cutting Bone-In Chops

1. First, cut through the chine bone using a handsaw. The chine bone holds the muscle to the backbone. This bone should be completely severed but not cut away from the meat. Use short, sawing strokes.

2. Use the guiding hand to hold the chine bone away from the meat. Work with the tip of a boning knife to make smooth strokes along the feather bones, cutting the meat cleanly away from them. Continue cutting until the chine bone and the feather bones are completely released from the meat.

3. Cut between each rib bone with a scimitar or chef's knife to make individual chops. The cut should be very clean to create a smooth surface on the chops. Once cut, the meaty portion of rib chops from pork, lamb, and venison can be shaped using the technique described for medallions from a beef tenderloin on page 103.

Use a handsaw to remove the chine bone (step 1).

Make smooth strokes along the feather bones (step 2).

Cut into chops (step 3).

Poultry

Trussing and disjointing poultry are common fabrication techniques. Trussing a bird gives it a smooth, compact shape and helps it cook more evenly. It is a common first step in roasting recipes.

Chicken and other young birds are easy to disjoint, and the skills necessary to halve and quarter a whole bird, as well as make a suprême, should be second nature to a professional chef. The younger the bird, the easier it is to cut up, as its bones are not completely hardened. The size and breed of the bird has some bearing on how easy or difficult it is to fabricate; chickens are generally far simpler to cut up than are pheasant, for example, because the tendons and ligaments in chickens are less well-developed than in game birds.

A poultry suprême is a semiboneless breast, usually from a chicken, pheasant, partridge, or duck. It is so named because it is considered the best ("supreme") portion. If the skin is removed from the suprême, the cut may be referred to as a *côtelette*. If the wing is removed entirely, the result is a boneless breast. Suprêmes and boneless breasts are typically sautéed, pan-fried, poached, or grilled.

Trussing Poultry

1. Place the bird to be trussed breast side up on a work surface. Cut a piece of kitchen string long enough to wrap around the bird twice lengthwise. Pass the string under both drumsticks, then loop the string around the end of each drumstick and cross it to make an X between the legs.

2. Pull the string to draw the legs together and then pull the string toward the tail. Next, pass both ends of the string tightly under the drumsticks to draw them close to the bird's body.

3. Pull the string over the joints that connect the drumsticks to the thighs. Continue pulling the string along the side of the bird's body and over the wings, tucking the wings in neatly. Turn the bird over onto its breast and tie the ends of the string securely underneath the backbone at the neck opening. Cut off any excess string.

Start by crossing the string to make an X (step 1).

Draw the drumsticks close to the body (step 2).

Knot the ends under the neck of the chicken (step 3).

Disjointing Poultry

1. Use a chef's knife or poultry shears to cut along each side of the backbone from the tail to the neck opening. If using a knife, insert the blade into the bird's cavity from the tail end while the bird is breast side up and cut through the rib cage with firm, steady motions. Pull the tail end of the bird upward slightly while cutting down along the second side of the backbone to make it easier to cut. Keep the blade close to the backbone, using as few cuts as possible, and avoid slashing the breast meat from inside the cavity for a neat appearance. Save the backbone for making broth.

2. Spread the bird open, skin side down. Use a boning knife to make a small cut just through the white cartilage located at the center of the breast at the top of the dark, hard, and flat keel bone. Grasp the keel bone firmly and pull it, along with the attached white cartilage, away from the breast meat. If needed, use the knife to remove any small pieces of cartilage or bone remaining on the breast meat. Cut the chicken into halves down the center of the breast.

3. Separate the leg and thigh from the breast and wing by cutting through the skin where it stretches between the top of the thigh and the bottom edge of the breast, exposing the joint, and cut through the joint. There should now be four large pieces.

4. If necessary, cut a quartered bird into smaller serving pieces: Place the legs skin side down on a cutting board. Look for a layer of fat over the joint connecting the drumstick and thigh and slice through the joint on the drumstick side of this layer (wiggle the leg to help locate the joint). Next, cut each of the half-breast portions into two pieces. Cut through the breast and the bones with a firm, downward slicing motion. To produce pieces with equal amounts of meat, do not cut the breast at the exact midpoint, but allot one-third of the breast to the portion with the wing attached and two-thirds of the breast to the other portion.

Cut in half and remove the backbone (step 1).   Remove the keel bone (step 2).   Separate the chicken into quarters (step 3).

Making Poultry Suprêmes

1. To remove the breast portions without cutting the bird in half, as explained on page 107 for disjointing, set the bird with the breast facing up. Use a boning knife to make two cuts, one on either side of the breast bone, working the tip of the knife around the bone. Continue to cut the breast pieces away from the rib cage, working on one side at a time. Cut with shallow strokes and hold the breast meat away from the bones while working. Try to cut as close to the bones as possible so none of the meat is left clinging to the bone. Cut through the tendons that hold the meat to the bones, especially where the wing joins the breast. Turn the chicken and repeat this process on the second side of the breast bone.

2. One wing joint is left attached to the breast meat for a classic suprême. Cut the first wing joint away before cutting the breast portions from the bird or after they have been cut away, as shown in the accompanying photograph. Locate the joint that connects the first and second sections of the wing and cut through the cartilage with a knife.

3. To remove the meat and skin from the wing bone, make a cut around the wing joint. Use the flat of the knife blade to hold the chicken steady while pulling the meat and skin off the bone.

4. When the meat and skin is scraped away from bones, especially wing bones for poultry or rib bones for chops, steaks, or crown roasts, the technique used to remove the meat and skin is known as "frenching," and it is done primarily for appearance. Use the edge of the blade of the boning knife to scrape the meat on the bone to expose the bone completely. If desired, cover the bones with foil to keep them white as the meat roasts or bakes.

Cut off the first section of the wing bone (step 2).

Cut the tendon to remove the skin (step 3).

Scraping the wing bone clean (frenching) (step 4).

Boneless Skinless Poultry Breast

Many dishes call for a boneless skinless poultry breast. This cut can be butterflied to create more surface area, perfect for paillards to grill or to make a cut that can be rolled around a filling. Once the breast is cut away from the carcass (follow the instructions in step 1 for making poultry suprêmes), use the tip of your boning knife to cut the wing bone where it joins the breast. Be sure to cut away any cartilage that remains. Save the wings to use in stocks or soups, or to make a variety of appetizers.

Some chefs remove the "tenderloin" from the breast at this point to save for another use. The tenderloin is held in place by a membrane, but it can be easily pulled away in one piece. You may need to use the tip of your boning or paring knife to take it completely off the breast. (For a better texture, remove the tendon from the tenderloin as follows: Hold the large end of the tendon tightly against your work surface. It can be found at the wide end of the tenderloin. You may find that a clean cloth helps you maintain a more secure grip. Then, holding the blade of your knife on top of the tendon so that it is nearly parallel with the work surface, press down with the blade and pull the tendon out with the other hand.)

Pull the skin away from the breast and trim any surface fat. If you wish to butterfly the piece, place your gloved hand on top of the breast and slice into the breast on the thicker side, making a cut that is parallel to the work surface. Continue to cut into the meat until you are about 1 inch from the thinner side. Open the breast like a book. The breast is ready to pound at this point, if necessary.

Rabbit

Rabbit is a relatively lean, mildly flavored meat that can be used for a number of preparations. The loin and rib sections tend to be drier than the legs, in much the same way that the chicken breast can be drier than the legs. First removing the legs and shoulder allows two different cooking methods to be applied to one rabbit—moist heat for the legs and dry heat for the loin—to achieve the most satisfactory results.

A fully disjointed rabbit is pictured here, including saddle, foreleg, shoulder sections, hind legs, liver, and kidneys. Any trim may be used to make a game stock, if desired.

CLOCKWISE FROM TOP LEFT A fully disjointed rabbit: hind legs, kidneys, foreleg and shoulder, saddle (center), foreleg and shoulder, and liver.

Disjointing a Rabbit

1. Spread open the belly cavity of the rabbit and pull out the kidney and liver. Sever any membrane attaching the liver to the cavity. The liver should be reserved for another use.

2. Pull the hind legs straight out from the body to expose the joints that connect the legs to the loin. Make a cut along the body to separate the leg meat from the loin. Cut com-pletely through the joint to remove the entire leg.

3. To separate the front legs and shoulder from the rest of the body, pull the leg away from the body. Use the flat side of your knife blade to steady the body as you pull. Cut as much meat away with the front legs and shoulders as possible and cut through the joints.

4. Trim the loin by cutting away the hind and front portions to produce the saddle. These sections have relatively little meat and are mainly bones. To cut through them cleanly, use the heel of your knife. Push down on the spine of the knife blade with the heel of your guiding hand to cut through the bones.

Remove the hind legs (step 2).

Cut the forelegs and shoulders away (step 3).

Trim the loin to produce the saddle (step 4).

Carving Roasted Meats and Poultry

The act of carving used to be considered a mark of honor. In Europe, in the Middle Ages, carving was considered an art form. Perfectly carved meats come from the roast juicy and tender, ready to be arranged on a plate. The traditional carving set includes a carving knife, a sharp knife with a guard at the hilt. In addition to a knife, a full set includes a carving fork, used to steady the roast as you work, and a steel to keep the blade sharp as you work.

Carving a boneless cut of meat requires some attention to the direction of the meat's grain. Carving meat against the grain means that you cut across the fibers in the meat for a smooth appearance and a more tender texture for the diner. Some boneless cuts are sliced at an angle to the meat, either to produce a slice of a particular shape and size, or to adjust for a specific cut of meat. Flank steak, for instance, is carved on an angle for the best texture. This angle assures that you cut against the grain.

Carving bone-in cuts calls for even more attention. Some roasts have bones that are easy to see. A rib roast, for example, has the bones on one side of the meat. To carve a rib roast (facing page), you cut across the meat (against the grain) up to the bone. Bone-in leg roasts and poultry present special challenges, since the bones are on the interior of the roast.

Whether you are carving meats in the kitchen or under the watchful eyes of your patrons in the dining room or on a buffet line, it is important to have a basic idea of where those hidden bones are located. We have illustrated three basic carving challenges here, for a rib roast (a beef roast is shown), a leg roast (a ham is shown), and a whole bird (a duck is shown). Whatever meat— beef, veal, lamb, or pork—or poultry—chicken, turkey, capon, or duck—you are carving, the basic placement of the bones is similar and the technique is simply adjusted to adapt to the size of the roast.

Be sure to wear clean, disposable food-handler's gloves when working with cooked foods to keep them safe. (For additional important information about safe food handling and gloves, see pages 52–53.)

Carving a Rib Roast

1. This carving method can also be used for a rack of veal or lamb. Lay the rib roast on its side. Using a sharp meat slicer, make a horizontal cut from the outer edge up to the rib bones. Use a kitchen fork to hold the meat steady while cutting. The cut should be parallel to the cutting surface.

2. Hold the knife vertically rather than horizontally to make a cut along the bones to free the slice of meat. Use the knife tip to cut the slice of meat away from the bone. Store the slice cut side up, if necessary, to prevent juice loss.

Make parallel cuts from the outer edge toward the bones (step 1).

Bone-In Leg Roasts

The same basic procedure demonstrated on a ham here can also be applied to other leg cuts (leg of lamb or venison, for example). Two major muscles, known as the inner and outer rounds or the top and bottom rounds, are attached to the leg. The top (or outer) round is larger and has a more pronounced curve.

Remember to reserve the ham bone and any wholesome trim for other uses. The bone can be used to flavor bean or lentil soups and stews and to make a rich broth. Lean trim can be used to make garnishes for soups, sauces, omelets, braises, and forcemeat items such as pâtés and terrines, and to prepare spreads, meat salads, and mousses.

Carving a Ham

1. Holding the ham steady, use a slicer to trim away the excess fat cover. The amount trimmed away is a matter of preference, but most diners today favor a clean trim. Trim away the meat from the end of the bone. Set the ham down on a cutting surface. If necessary, cut away a thin slice to help it stay stable.

2. Make parallel cuts beginning at the shank and working toward the opposite end of the ham. The slices will be relatively small when you begin. Cut vertically through the meat until the knife blade touches the bone and use the edge of the blade to cut the slice free from the bone.

3. When the slices become very large, begin to cut the meat at a slight angle, first from the left side, then from the right side, alternating until the leg is entirely sliced.

Begin from the shank end; alternate sides when slices become large.

Whole Roasted Poultry

When a guest orders roast duck, the duck is halved and the bones removed so that the leg portion has only the drumstick bone and the breast portion a single wing bone. They are nestled together so that the boneless breast and thigh meat overlap. The guest can simply cut into the meat without having to work around bones.

Carving and Presenting Roast Duck

1. Cut the legs away from the body at the point where the leg meets the breast and pull away the leg to reach the ball-and-socket joint. Remove the thigh bone from the leg by simultaneously pulling up the bone and cutting the meat away with the tip of a boning knife.

2. Carve the breast away from the rib cage with little trim loss by running the blade edge as close to the bones as possible. Cut through the tendons holding the breast meat to the bones to separate the breast from the carcass.

3. Pull the thigh bone up and away from the thigh meat. Use the tip of the knife as pictured to separate the bone at the leg joint. Overlap the leg and breast portions for one style of presentation: Place the leg portion on the plate first and set the breast portion onto the leg so that the large, boneless portions of breast and thigh overlap, with the drumstick bone and the wing bone on opposite sides.

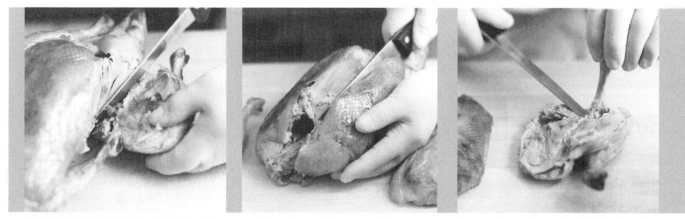

Cut away the legs where they meet the breast (step 1).

Cut the duck breast from the bird (step 2).

Separate the duck leg at the joint with the knife tip (step 3).

CUTTING TECHNIQUES FOR FISH AND SHELLFISH

5

Fish and shellfish are popular on most menus and demand continues to grow, even in the face of reports about toxins in fish, problems with farm-raised fish, and the perils of overfishing. The benefits of fish in our diets appear to outweigh the drawbacks.

Seafood makes very specific demands on the chef. Bivalves (clams, oysters, and mussels) are shucked to serve on the half shell or to cook. Shrimp are often peeled and deveined. Lobster is disjointed and cracked to get at the meat inside the shell.

The bones and shells from seafood can be used to make soups and stocks. However, because fish is so costly, you should be completely confident in your skills or the skills of your staff. Even though you can use edible trim, bones, and shells to make other dishes, those dishes alone can't make up for the money that is lost when you consistently get only 6 portions from a fish that is supposed to yield 8 portions.

If you can cut your own fish properly, you can be assured of good quality, portion sizes that meet specifications, and a lower overall food cost.

Round Fish

Fillets are one of the most common ways to fabricate a fish. These boneless and (usually) skinless fish pieces can be sautéed, grilled, baked, formed into paupiettes (pieces of fish fillet rolled into a cork shape), or cut into tranches (portion-sized slices of fillet) or goujonettes (strips of fillet about the size of an index finger).

One basic fish fabrication technique, shown here, is filleting a round fish. For more details on how to fillet flat fish and other fish fabrication techniques, read *The Professional Chef, 8th edition,* pages 491 to 506.

Filleting a Round Fish

1. Lay the fish on a cutting board with the backbone parallel to the work surface and the head on the same side as the hand holding your knife. Cut behind the head and gill plates. Angle the knife so that the cutting motion is down and away from the body. This cut does not cut the head of the fish away from the body.

2. Without removing the knife, turn it so that the cutting edge is pointing toward the tail of the fish. Position the knife so that the handle is lower than the tip of the blade. This improves the yield by keeping the knife's edge aimed at the bones rather than the flesh.

3. Run the blade down the length of the fish, cutting against the backbone. Avoid sawing the knife back and forth. If you cut evenly and smoothly, you should actually split the tail. Once the fillet is freed from the bones, lay it skin side down on the work surface or in a hotel pan. Lift the fillet with both hands to keep it intact.

4. After turning the fish over, insert the blade just underneath the backbone. Lay your guiding hand flat on top of the second fillet to keep the fish stable. Hold the knife parallel to the cutting surface. Using the same smooth cutting motion, run the blade along the entire length of the fillet. Angle the cutting edge upward very slightly so that you are cutting against the bone to increase the usable yield on the second fillet.

5. Remove the belly bones with smooth, cutting strokes just underneath the bones to cut them cleanly away. Cut away the remnants of the backbone by running the blade just underneath its line, lifting it up and away from the fillet as you cut.

6. To remove the skin, lay the fillet parallel to the edge of the cutting surface, with the tail to the left if you are right-handed and to the right if left-handed. Hold the tail firmly with the guiding hand and carefully insert the knife between the skin and the flesh. Holding the knife so that the cutting edge is cutting against the skin, pull the skin taut with the guiding hand while cutting the fillet free from the skin. The motion should be relatively smooth, with a very slight sawing motion.

7. Remove the pin bones at this point—locate them by running a fingertip over the fillet. Use pliers or tweezers to pull out the bones, pulling them out in the direction of the head of the fillet (working with the grain) to avoid ripping the flesh.

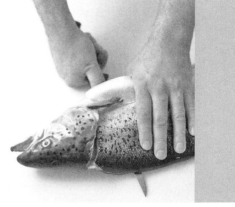

Cut behind the head and gill plates (step 1).　　Cut toward the tail to remove the first fillet (step 2).　　Repeat on the other side (step 4).

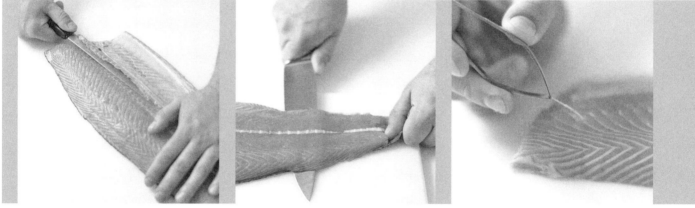

Remove the belly bones (step 5).　　Pull the skin taut and cut the fillet free (step 6).　　Remove the pin bones (step 7).

Lobster

Lobster should be alive when you purchase it. The first step in preparing a lobster for boiling or steaming is to kill it. Lobsters can also be split before they are broiled or baked. The edible meat can be removed from a cooked lobster to produce a large tail portion, intact claw sections, and smaller pieces from the knuckles and legs.

Preparing Live Lobster to Cook

1. Leave the bands on the lobster's claws and lay it stomach side down on a work surface. Insert the tip of a chef's knife into base of head.

2. Pull the knife all the way down through the shell, splitting the head in half.

3. Split the tail by reversing the direction of the lobster and positioning the tip of a chef's knife at the point of the initial cut. Cut through the shell of the tail section.

4. The lobster's tomalley and coral (if any) should be reserved and used as an ingredient in stuffings, sauces, or butters. Split lobsters can be stuffed and broiled, baked, or grilled.

Removing the Meat from a Cooked Lobster

1. Wearing wire mesh gloves or disposable food-handling gloves, hold the tail section securely in one hand; hold the body of the lobster with the other. Twist the hands in opposite directions, pulling the tail away from the body.

2. Use scissors to cut down both sides of the underside of the lobster tail. Pull away the flap of shell and then pull the tail meat out of the shell with gloved fingers—it should come away in one piece.

3. Use the heel of the knife, pliers, lobster or nut crackers to crack the claw shell. Pull away enough of the shell to get access to the meat inside the shell. Pull it out gently using the fingers to pry the shell away from the meat. The claw meat should also come out in a single piece, retaining the shape of the claw.

4. Even though the meat in the legs and knuckles is in smaller pieces, use it to make salads, soups, stuffings, and other preparations where the appearance of the lobster meat is less important. Use a chef's knife to cut through the lobster knuckles. Pull out the knuckle meat.

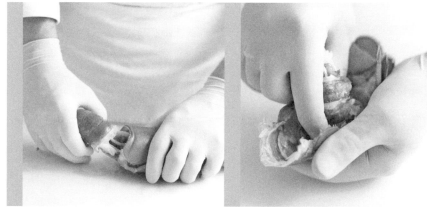

Twist off the tail (step 1).

Cut the tail open and pull out the meat in one piece (step 2).

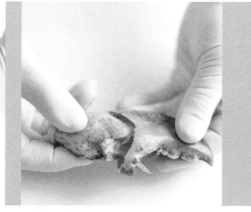

Crack the shell and pull out the claw meat (step 3).

Shrimp

Shrimp can be cooked and served in the shell, typically for cold presentations such as cocktails, salads, or on a raw bar. Shrimp served hot, whether it is sautéed, grilled, or fried, should be cleaned before it is cooked. Cleaned shrimp have had their shells removed, a process known as peeling, and their intestinal vein removed, a process known as deveining.

Cleaning Shrimp

1. Shrimp shells pull easily away from the shrimp meat. The shells can be reserved for other uses such as making shrimp stock, bisque, and shellfish butters. The vein, which runs along the edge of the shrimp, is easy to locate. Lay the peeled shrimp on a work surface, with the curved outer edge of the shrimp on the same side as cutting hand. Slice into the shrimp with a paring or utility knife. The cut should be quite shallow for deveining, deeper if you are butterflying the shrimp.

2. After you have made the cut, use the edge of your knife blade to scrape out the intestinal tract, a dark vein that runs along the back of the shrimp. Twist the knife blade to pull the vein out and away from the shrimp.

3. Instead of cutting into the shrimp, you can also remove the vein without cutting the shrimp. After you have peeled the shrimp, use a toothpick or skewer to "hook" the vein. Pull the vein out completely. The shrimp is now ready to poach for shrimp cocktail, or for other presentations.

Slice the outer curve to expose the vein (step 1).   Scrape out the vein (step 2).   Or hook the vein with a toothpick and pull it out (step 3).

Soft-Shelled Crabs

A seasonal favorite, soft-shelled crabs are considered a great delicacy. They are not especially difficult to clean once their various parts are identified.

Soft-shelled crabs are commonly prepared by sautéing or pan-frying, and the shell may be eaten along with the meat.

Cleaning Soft-Shelled Crabs

1. Peel back the pointed shell and scrape away the gill filament on each side.

2. Cut the eyes and mouth away from the head just behind the eyes, and squeeze gently to force out the green bubble, which has an unpleasant flavor.

3. Bend back the tail flap (or apron) and pull with a slight twisting motion. The intestinal vein is drawn out of the body at the same time.

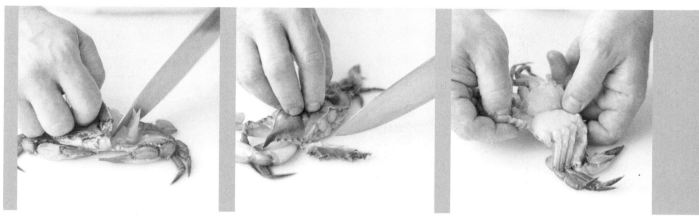

Remove the gills from each side (step 1).   Push the green bubble out from the head (step 2).   Pull the tail flap away (step 3).

Clams and Oysters

Clams and oysters are often served raw on the half shell, so it is important to be able to open them with ease. In addition, freshly shucked oysters and clams are often used for cooked dishes such as oysters Rockefeller and clams casino.

Clams and oysters have a top and bottom shell held together by a hinge. The method for opening clams calls for the edge of a clam knife to be inserted between the shells. To open an oyster, insert the tip of an oyster knife directly into the hinge.

Scrub all mollusks well with a brush under cold running water before opening them. Any shellfish that remain open when tapped must be discarded because they are dead. If the shell feels unusually heavy or light, it should be checked as it could be empty or contain clay or sand.

Be sure to reserve any juices; these are sometimes referred to as "liquor" and they add great flavor to soups, stews, and stocks. Filter the liquor through a paper filter or sieve lined with a triple thickness of cheesecloth to remove any bits of shell before adding it to another dish.

Opening Oysters

1. Wear a wire mesh glove to hold the oyster. Position the oyster so that the hinged side is facing outward. Work the tip of an oyster knife into the hinge, holding the upper and lower shells together, and twist it to break open the hinge.

2. Once the shell opens, slide the knife over the inside of the top shell to release the oyster from the shell. Make a similar stroke to release the oyster from the bottom shell.

Hold the oyster with the hinge facing out (step 1).   Release the oyster from the bottom shell (step 2).

Opening Clams

1. Wear a wire mesh glove to hold the clam. Position the clam so that the hinged side is facing inward. Work the side of a clam knife into the seam between the upper and lower shells.

The fingers of the gloved hand can be used both to help guide the knife and to give extra force. Twist the blade slightly, as if turning a key in a lock, to pry open the shell.

2. When the clamshell opens, slide the knife over the inside of the top shell to release the clam from the shell. Make a similar stroke to release the clam from the bottom shell.

Twist a clam knife like a key in a lock between the shells of a clam (step 1).

Release the clam from the top shell (step 2).

6

HAND TOOLS FOR MEASURING, MIXING, AND BAKING

One of the most versatile "tools" in the professional kitchen is a recipe. Chefs use recipes for far more than just making a dish—they use them to organize their work, control costs, and improve every aspect of the dish, from its appearance to its flavor.

Learning to use recipes effectively means mastering some basic skills, many of which we have already presented in this book. No matter how recipes list ingredients, to a cook, that means peeling, trimming, and cutting.

Recipes have specific measurements for reasons beyond the obvious purpose of letting you know how much to put in the pan or the bowl. Adhering to your recipe's measurements means that you will be able to accurately order foods so that you have an appropriate inventory of goods on hand, that you will be able to produce the right amount of food, and that your portions and servings will be consistent in flavor, texture, appearance, and size.

Tools for measuring and portioning are basics in any professional kitchen. Measuring tools such as spoons, cups, pitchers, and scales can measure ingredients as well as portions. Tools like scoops, ladles, and pastry bags can be used for portioning and during the cooking process. Thermometers are special measuring tools that every chef must be able to use properly. Maintaining the right temperature means that foods will have better flavors, colors, and textures. It also means that a chef can be confident that the foods served to guests have been handled with safety in mind.

Tools for Measuring

Accurate measurements are crucial to recipes. In order to keep costs in line and ensure consistency of quality and quantity, ingredients and portion sizes must be measured correctly each time a recipe is made.

Ingredients are purchased and used according to one of three measuring conventions: count, volume, or weight. They may be purchased according to one system and measured for use in a recipe according to another.

Count is a measurement of whole items as one would purchase them. The terms *each, bunch,* and *dozen* all indicate units of count measure. If the individual item has been processed, graded, or packaged according to established standards, count can be a useful, accurate way to measure ingredients. It is less accurate for ingredients requiring some advance preparation or without any established standards for purchasing. Garlic cloves illustrate the point well. If a recipe calls for 2 garlic cloves, the intensity of garlic in the dish will change depending upon whether the cloves you use are large or small.

Converting Between U.S. and Metric Measurement Systems

The metric system, used throughout most of the world, is a decimal system, meaning that it is based on multiples of 10. The gram is the basic unit of weight, the liter is the basic unit of volume, and the meter is the basic unit of length. Prefixes added to the basic units indicate larger or smaller units. For instance, a kilogram is 1,000 grams, a milliliter is $\frac{1}{1000}$ of a liter, and a centimeter is $\frac{1}{100}$ of a meter.

The U.S. system, familiar to most Americans, uses ounces and pounds to measure weight, and teaspoons, tablespoons, fluid ounces, cups, pints, quarts, and gallons to measure volume. Unlike the metric system, the U.S. system is not based on multiples of a particular number, so it is not as simple to increase or decrease quantities.

Most modern measuring equipment is capable of measuring in both U.S. and metric units. If, however, a recipe is written in a system of measurement for which you do not have the proper measuring equipment, you will need to convert to the other system.

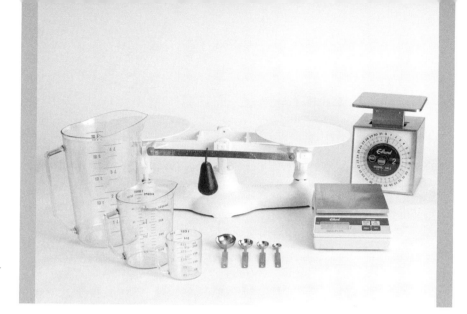

CLOCKWISE FROM CENTER Balance scale, spring or portion scale, digital scale, measuring spoons, and graduated measuring cups and pitchers.

To convert ounces to grams and pounds to kilograms: Multiply ounces by 28.35 to determine grams; divide pounds by 2.2 to determine kilograms

To convert grams to ounces or pounds: Divide grams by 28.35 to determine ounces; divide grams by 453.59 to determine pounds

To convert fluid ounces to milliliters: Multiply fluid ounces by 29.58 to determine milliliters

To convert milliliters to fluid ounces: Divide milliliters by 29.58 to determine fluid ounces

Metric Prefixes

kilo = 1,000 (so, a kilogram is 1000 grams)

hecto = 100 (so, a hectogram is 100 grams)

deka = 10 (so, a dekagram is 10 grams)

deci = 1/10 (so, a decigram is .1 gram)

centi = 1/100 (so, a centigram is .01 gram)

milli = 1/1000 (so, a milligram is .001 gram)

Measures and Conversions

Weight Measures Conversions between U.S. and Metric Measurement Systems

U.S.	METRIC*
¼ ounce	8 grams
½ ounce	15 grams
1 ounce	30 grams
4 ounces	115 grams
8 ounces (½ pound)	225 grams
16 ounces (1 pound)	450 grams
32 ounces (2 pounds)	900 grams
40 ounces (2¼ pounds)	1 kilogram

*Metric values have been rounded.

Volume Measures Conversions between U.S. and Metric Measurement Systems

U.S.	METRIC*
1 teaspoon	5 milliliters
1 tablespoon	15 milliliters
1 fluid ounce (2 tablespoons)	30 milliliters
2 fluid ounces (¼ cup)	60 milliliters
8 fluid ounces (1 cup)	240 milliliters
16 fluid ounces (1 pint)	480 milliliters
32 fluid ounces (1 quart)	950 milliliters (.95 liter)
128 fluid ounces (1 gallon)	3.75 liters

*Metric values have been rounded.

Volume Versus Weight

Confusion can arise between weight and volume measures when ounces are the unit of measure. It is important to remember that weight is measured in ounces, but volume is measured in fluid ounces. A standard volume measuring cup is equal to 8 fluid ounces, but the contents of the cup may not always weigh 8 ounces. One cup (8 fluid ounces) of cornflakes weighs only 1 ounce, but 1 cup (8 fluid ounces) of peanut butter weighs 9 ounces. Water is the only substance for which it can be safely assumed that 1 fluid ounce equals 1 ounce. For all other ingredients, when the amount is expressed in ounces, weigh it; when the amount is expressed in fluid ounces, measure it with an accurate liquid (or volume) measuring tool.

Converting Volume Measures

FLUID OUNCES	GALLONS	QUARTS	PINTS	CUPS	TABLESPOONS	TEASPOONS
128 fluid ounces	1 gallon	4 quarts	8 pints	16 cups	256 tablespoons	768 teaspoons
32 fluid ounces	1/4 gallon	1 quart	2 pints	4 cups	64 tablespoons	192 teaspoons
16 fluid ounces	1/8 gallon	1/2 quart	1 pint	2 cups	32 tablespoons	96 teaspoons
8 fluid ounces	NA	1/4 quart	1/2 pint	1 cup	16 tablespoons	48 teaspoons
1 fluid ounce	NA	NA	NA	1/8 cup	2 tablespoons	6 teaspoons

Tools for Measuring Volume

Volume is a measurement of the space occupied by a solid, liquid, or gas. The terms *teaspoon (tsp)*, *tablespoon (tbsp)*, *fluid ounce (fl oz)*, *cup (c)*, *pint (pt)*, *quart (qt)*, *gallon (gal)*, *milliliter (mL)*, and *liter (L)* all indicate units of volume measure. Graduated containers, such as measuring cups, and utensils for which the volume is known, such as such as a 2-ounce ladle or a teaspoon, are used to measure volume.

Volume measurements are best suited to liquids, although they are also used for solids, especially spices, in small amounts. Tools used for measuring volume are not always as precise as necessary, especially if you must often increase or decrease a recipe. Volume measuring tools need not conform to any regulated standards. Therefore, the amount of an ingredient measured with one set of spoons, cups, or pitchers could be quite different from the amount measured with another set.

Measuring Liquids Properly

To measure liquids, use graduated measuring cups or pitchers and fill to the desired level. To be sure to measure accurately, bend down until the level mark on the measure is at eye level. The measuring utensil must be sitting on a level surface for an accurate measurement.

Measuring Pitchers Pitchers are (usually) used to measure multiple cups or large amounts of milliliters and liters. They are often used to measure fluids and have sturdy handles to allow you to lift the vessel and its heavy contents. Pitchers are often graduated, allowing you to measure amounts that are a fraction of the pitcher's total capacity, (for example, a gallon pitcher might have four divisions, each section equal to a quart). Pitchers are available in gallon, half gallon, quart, and pint sizes.

Measuring Cups Cups come in sets, generally, and are used with the U.S. measurement system. Sets can include 1 cup, ½ cup, ⅓ cup, ¼ cup, and possibly ⅛ cup measuring vessels. These are used to measure both wet and dry ingredients.

Measuring Spoons Measuring spoons are useful to measure small amounts of ingredients used to season, flavor, or leaven foods. Spoon sets come with tablespoon, teaspoon, ½ teaspoon, and ¼ teaspoon measures, and may include ½ tablespoon and ⅛ teaspoon measures as well.

Tools for Measuring Weight

Weight is a measurement of the mass or heaviness of a solid, liquid, or gas. The terms *ounce (oz), pound (lb), gram (g),* and *kilogram (kg)* all indicate units of weight measure. Scales are used to measure weight, and they must meet specific standards for accuracy. In professional kitchens, weight is usually the preferred type of measurement because it is easier to attain accuracy with weight than with volume.

The key to accurate weight measurement is a functioning scale that has been properly set up. To measure ingredients on a scale, first prepare them as directed by the recipe—chop nuts, mince garlic, grate cheeses, and so forth.

Set a container on the scale to hold the ingredient and reset the scale to zero (known as "tare") or balance it properly (for more information, read about specific scales below). Then add the ingredient to the container until you have the desired amount.

Balance Scale A balance scale has two arms. When the weight on each side of the scale is equal, then the arms are balanced. You can tell that they are balanced because they are level. To use a balance scale, first add a container to the right side of

The chef is using a spring scale to weigh a steak.

the scale to hold your ingredient. Add weight to the left-hand side of the scale, either by sliding a marker along a scale for small amounts, or by adding weights directly to the platform on the left side. Then, add the ingredient to the right side as needed until the arms are level and in balance.

Spring Scale This type of scale works by placing a spring beneath a flat surface. The food is placed on the surface and the spring presses down. A dial turns to reflect the amount of pressure applied to the spring. To zero the scale, place your measuring receptacle on the scale and twist the dial until the needle aligns with the zero.

This type of scale requires no additional weights, but the spring can wear out over time and lose calibration. Additionally, the dial can lose calibration, but this is easier to fix than the spring. This scale allows extremely accurate measurements, and depending on the strength of the spring, can easily measure milligrams.

Digital Scale Digital scales measure the amount of pressure applied to the measuring surface, much like a spring scale. The digital scale is more accurate, though, and there is less chance of misreading the weight of an item. Digital scales have a readout that gives accurate readings, sometimes down to very small increments. To zero the scale, place your measuring receptacle on the scale and press the zero or tare button.

Tools for Measuring Temperature

You will need to measure the temperature of food throughout your work in a kitchen. Serving safe food requires that products be heated to specific internal temperatures. Cooking oil temperature needs to be monitored in a fritteur for frying small batches of food. Water needs to be heated or cooled to specific temperatures to achieve the desired dough temperature in the bakery. Each of these measurements requires a thermometer that is accurate and easy to use. There are two basic types: analog and digital.

Analog (Instant-Read) Thermometers These thermometers work on the principle that things expand when you heat them. The expanding action causes a needle on the face of the thermometer to turn and gives you a temperature reading.

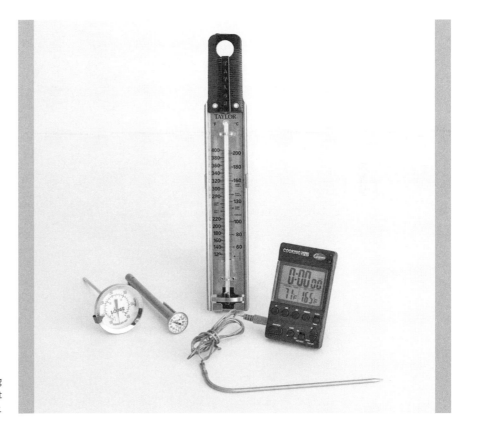

FROM LEFT Large and small dial analog thermometers, a candy and deep-fat thermometer, and a digital probe thermometer.

You can calibrate analog thermometers by placing them in ice water (a mixture of ice and water, not just cold water) and turning a nut just below the face of the thermometer until the needle is in the correct position to reflect the water's temperature (32°F). It's ineffective to calibrate the thermometer in boiling water because water boils at different temperatures depending on the altitude.

Digital Thermometers Digital thermometers measure the temperature of a food by measuring the amount of resistance a current receives as it passes through the metal end of the device. A computer chip then translates the measured resistance into a temperature using a simple program written onto the chip. These thermometers cannot be calibrated because of the nature of their program. They need new batteries on occasion.

A candy thermometer is used to measure the temperature of sugar syrup.

Candy Thermometers Analog candy thermometers have larger faces than instant-reads and have a clip that allows them to attach to the lip of a pot. They measure a much wider range of temperatures (for example, sugar can heat up past 500°F) and have additional descriptors on the dial face that refer to the stage of melted sugar as it cooks.

Meat Thermometers Meat thermometers have a long needle that is inserted into a piece of meat before cooking. A cord connects the needle to a readout attached to the front of the oven with a magnet. This allows for closing the oven door and monitoring the meat's temperature. Generally, the thermometer can be preset with a desired temperature, and an alarm beeps when the temperature is reached.

Oven Thermometers An oven thermometer is made to be placed inside the oven to allow a cook to monitor the temperature (ovens can often run hotter or colder than the temperature to which they are set). The thermometer is a large dial with feet and a hook at the top (it can stand on the rack or hang from the rack).

Freezer and Refrigerator Thermometers These bulb thermometers function on the same principle as an analog thermometer and are placed inside a refrigerator or freezer to monitor the internal temperature.

Tools for Mixing and Baking

Hand tools used for mixing ingredients are simple and straightforward in their design and function. Spoons and whisks are used to mix batters, whip egg whites or cream, blend mixtures to use as fillings or toppings, as well as to portion foods and serve them. Mortars and pestles are used to mix sauces and to grind spices. Some special baking tools, including bench scrapers and pastry bags, also have multiple functions. In addition to their use in creating decorative fillings and toppings for desserts, pastry bags are also used to portion foods, as are portioning scoops and ladles. Bench and bowl scrapers are useful to scrape things out of bowls or to lift things from a cutting board so you can add them to a bowl or pan. Stiff doughs like pie crust or pasta doughs call for rolling pins.

Spoons

A professional-quality kitchen spoon may have a slotted or perforated head, in addition to the standard solid head, and is an extremely large version of the household version. Spoons are used for stirring, mixing, and serving items. Spoons may be made from metal, plastic (ideally heatproof for use when mixing on the stove top in a pan or pot), and wood.

A wooden spoon has enough texture to make it easy to blend and cream ingredients together. These spoons should be handled properly. If they are left in contact with a very hot surface or an open flame, they can burn or scorch. Wash wooden spoons by hand, not in an automatic dishwasher. The high temperatures and chemicals could dry the wood out enough to permit it to split or crack.

Metal spoons may have a solid bowl, making them appropriate for serving sauces or foods that are soft. Slotted or perforated spoons are used to lift foods out of a liquid.

Wood's texture helps soften and cream foods.

A slotted spoon is used to drain and strain foods such as slaw.

Whisks

A ball- or teardrop-shaped mass of wires extrudes from the whisk's handle, allowing it to stir, mix, and aerate batters and mixtures. The thickness or thinness of the wires dictates the flexibility of the whisk. The more flexible whisks are ideal for thin batters while stiffer whisks work well with thick batters.

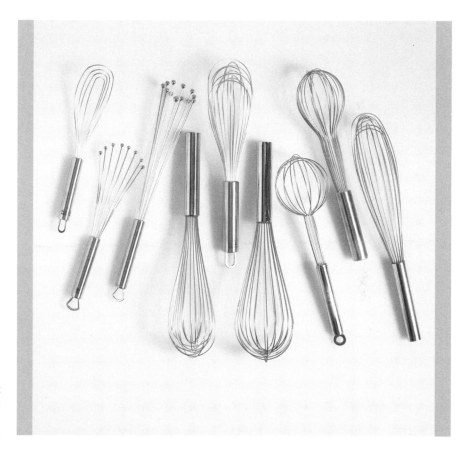

LEFT TO RIGHT Flat (roux) whisk, flat (roux) whisk with ball bearings, French (sauce) whisk with ball bearings, balloon whisks (3), round balloon whisks (2), and French (sauce) whisk.

Bench Scraper

Use these tools to clean the surface of your workspace, do some simple cutting tasks (portioning dough, chopping nuts, etc.), or lift and transfer items. The scraper is usually composed of a straight handle constructed of wood or plastic and a rectangular (dull) blade of metal.

Bowl Scraper

Bowl scrapers are used to scrape bowls as you work. They are prominently used when working with a mixer, where you need to scrape down the sides as you progressively add ingredients, which ensures a more uniform mixture. Scrapers are also used to thoroughly remove a batter or dough from the mixing bowl. Scrapers are generally constructed of a flexible plastic, with a flat, thick end serving as a handle and a curved end serving as the "blade."

Mortar and Pestle

Dating back as far back as the Stone Age, the mortar and pestle is one of the most basic tools in our repertoire, along with the knife. There are two parts to this hand-powered grinding device: the mortar, a concave surface such as a bowl that holds the food while the pestle, a rod with a curved end, is pressed and rubbed against the food. The mortar and pestle are used to grind almost any foodstuff to a desired texture.

Mortars and Pestles

The great appeal of this tool is the way it lets you control the texture of the food as precisely as you can control its flavor. There is a measurable difference between a pesto made by rubbing the basil in a marble mortar with a wooden pestle. That's been the tradition in southern France for hundreds of years. If you try it yourself, you'll see why.

It is satisfying to make foods using "primitive" tools. You feel the food and the tool. You hear the sounds. And when you are done, you can taste the difference.

CHEF MARK AINSWORTH, THE CULINARY INSTITUTE OF AMERICA

The device has developed into a range of styles, according to the traditional materials available and the types of grinding tasks important in a particular cuisine. One of the oldest mortar and pestles comes from the Tehuacan Valley in Mexico and dates back some 6,000 years, alongside the "discovery" of corn. The Mexican *molcajete y teyelote* is constructed of lava stone and is the traditional equipment for preparing *pico de gallo,* a tradional salsa (or condiment). A *metate y metlapil* is a variation: the mortar is a curved plate and the pestle is a bellowed rolling pin. This device was traditionally used to make flour.

Japanese cooks use a *suribachi* (a textured earthenware bowl) and *surigoki* (a wooden dowel) both pictured below. Smooth mortars and pestles are constructed from granite in Thailand, while in southern France a granite mortar and wooden pestle are the traditional tools for making *pistou,* a preparation similar to pesto. Mortar and pestle sets were commonly found in European apothecaries, where they were used to grind medicines for prescriptions.

Grinding sesame seeds in a *suribachi.*

Rolling Pins

These tools can be as simple as a long, cylindrical dowel, or a thick, hollowed dowel with a pair of handles attached at each end by ball bearings. Regardless of appearances, a rolling pin's function is the forming, flattening, and spreading of doughs to an even and consistent thickness. A springerle is a textured pin that creates a pattern

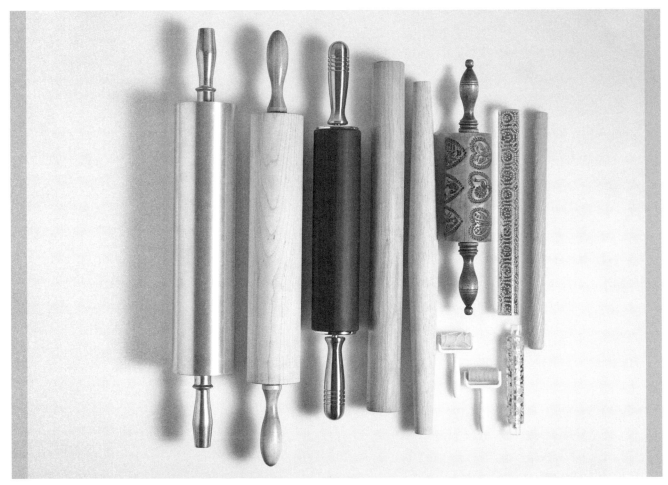

LEFT TO RIGHT Ball-bearing rolling pins (metal, wood, and silicone), French pins (straight and tapered), and a variety of patterned pins and pastry wheels.

along the dough's surface. Rolling pins are commonly made from wood, but may also be constructed from alternate materials that stay cooler while rolling, which helps keep the dough at the proper working temperature. They can be textured or plain; tapered or straight. Regardless of appearance, rolling pins need to be kept clean and free of dough. After each use, wipe the pin clean with a warm, damp towel. If the pin uses bearings, it should not be submerged in water because the bearings will rust and ruin the pin. Specific styles of rolling pins are described below:

Rod-and-bearing rolling pins consist of a cylinder made of hard wood with a steel rod inserted through the middle. The rod is fixed in place with ball bearings and handles at either end. These heavy pins are used to roll large amounts of dough and stiff doughs. Pins of this style are also available with a cylinder made of stainless steel or marble and are available in lengths up to 18 inches.

Straight (or French) rolling pins are straight, thick dowels. They were traditionally made of hardwood and now are also available in nylon. These pins are typically 1½ to 2 inches in diameter and 18 to 20 inches long. Because they don't have handles, they allow more sensitivity to the thickness and evenness of the dough while rolling it out.

Tapered rolling pins are thicker in the center, tapering evenly to both ends. They are usually about 2¾ inches in diameter at the center and 22 inches long. Their tapered design makes them most useful for rolling rounds of dough to line pie and tart pans, as well as for rolling pizzas.

Marzipan and basket-weave rolling pins have patterned surfaces to create impressions on marzipan for décor. These pins are made as rod-and-bearing pins or simply plain cylinders made of nylon or plastic.

Springerle rolling pins are made of wood or plastic resin. They have ornate and intricate pictures or designs in relief and are traditionally used to imprint springerle or gingerbread cookie doughs before baking. Springerle plaques are also available; the plaque is simply pressed into the rolled dough to imprint it before baking.

Pastry Bags and Tips

There are mixtures in the bakeshop and kitchen that are too soft or too wet to effectively form and shape. A pastry bag allows you to pipe soft, pliable substances such as whipped cream, mashed potatoes, or pâte à choux into specific shapes and forms. Commonly, pastry bags are made of canvas, but single-use plastic pastry bags are popular. In a pinch, a heavy-duty plastic bag such as a freezer bag can be used. Pastry bags are shaped like triangles, with a mouth on the shorter open side. A metal or plastic tip can be place at the smaller open end of the bag before adding the food. Different tips create specific effects.

Pastry or piping bags are used as portioning tools. Here one is used to portion the filling onto wonton wrappers.

Portioning Scoops

Portioning scoops are used to portion foods such as salads or ice cream for service or to portion out batters or doughs. Mechanical scoops have a lever to operate a blade that sweeps over the inside of the scoop's bowl to release the food. Scoops are made in a variety of standard sizes that are numbered according to their volume. The higher the number, the smaller the volume: A #16 scoop makes larger cookies than a #30 or #24 scoop. You might use a #16 scoop to portion meatballs and a #6 for a hamburger.

Portioning scoops produce consistent sizes for even baking.

Summary

All great craftsmen and artists rely on their tools. Finding the right tool for the task is a more complex activity than simply picking up the nearest paint brush or chisel and beginning to work. The way the tool is made, the way it fits your hand, the materials used in its construction, and the purpose for which it is intended all play a part in producing the best possible tool for an individual chef.

When the right tools are matched with the right hands, the results are almost magical. When you watch a professional magic act, you may find yourself awed by the trick. You are a willing believer in the illusion created by the magician. If, however, you are a magician, you are no longer in awe of the trick itself; you are astonished instead by the skill and finesse of the magician—the ease, the apparent effortlessness of motion.

Chefs are a great deal like magicians. To the novice, the transformation of a carrot to a pile of perfectly even julienne is almost miraculous. To the seasoned chef, the miracle is the skill, the coordination, and the rhythm of the right tool in an accomplished hand.

Glossary

Alloy A homogeneous mixture of two or more metals.

Arkansas stone A hard, smooth stone quarried from the Ozark Mountains in Arkansas, U.S.A. Used for sharpening knives.

Balance The way that the weight in a knife is distributed between blade and handle. Balance point is where the blade meets the handle.

Blade The portion of a knife that is used for cutting, slicing, and chopping.

Bolster The thick band of steel between the body of the blade and the handle. Also referred to as the shank.

Boning knife A knife of varying length and flexibility used primarily in the butchering and fabrication of meat and poultry and sometimes fish.

Bronze An alloy of copper and tin.

Bronze Age The time in human history when bronze was the preferred metal for tools and knives, about 3500 B.C.E.

Carbon steel An alloy of carbon and steel used to make knife blades; it takes a good edge and resists discoloration and staining.

Carborundum stone A sharpening stone available in various "grits" to sharpen knives to the desired degree of fineness. A man-made abrasive material used in the manufacture of sharpening stones.

Carving knife A knife used to carve cooked meats.

Ceramic A very hard, nonmetallic mineral compound (usually clay) formed and hardened by firing at high temperatures.

Chef's knife An all-purpose knife used for chopping, slicing, and mincing. The blade is usually between 8 and 14 inches long. Also referred to as a French knife or cook's knife.

Chinese cleaver An all-purpose cleaver typically sharpened on one side of the blade.

Cleaver A cutting tool with a large, heavy blade; available in a range of sizes. Butcher's cleavers are heavy enough to cut through bones and joints.

Cross contamination The spread of bacteria or other pathogens from one food or surface to another through improper handling and sanitary procedures.

Diamond-impregnated steel or stone A sharpening or honing tool that has been produced with industrial-grade diamonds over the surface.

Edge The sharp part of the knife blade, running from tip to tang, that does the cutting.

Ergonomics The study of how work space and equipment design affect productivity.

Fillet knife A flexible-bladed knife used for filleting fish.

Flat-ground A knife edge formed by grinding an angle at the base of a uniformly thick blade as opposed to tapering the blade.

Forge To form metal through heating and hammering and then stabilize its properties through tempering.

French knife *See* Chef's knife.

Full tang An extension of the blade into the handle.

Grinding Creating an edge on a blade using a rotating abrasive surface, usually a belt or wheel.

Grit Degree of coarseness of a sharpening stone.

Guiding hand The hand holding the item to be cut and acting as a guide to the knife blade.

Guard (of a steel) The metal piece between the handle and the steel.

Hazard Analysis of Critical Control Points (HACCP) A method of preventing food-borne disease by identifying potentially hazardous "control points" in the flow of food products through the production process and designing the process to eliminate contamination.

Hand-finished Indicates that polishing and sharpening of the knife is done by a person, not on a machine.

Handle The part of the knife that is held. It may be made of various materials, including wood, plastic, wood impregnated with plastic, rubber-like compounds, and steel.

Heel The back edge of the knife closest to the handle, used for tough jobs where weight and strength are required, such as cutting hard vegetables, bones, or shells.

High-carbon stainless steel A metal that contains a high percentage of carbon (up to 1.5 percent) in relation to stainless steel. It may also contain iron, chromium, molybdenum, and/or vanadium.

Hollow-ground edge An edge formed by grinding into the blade at a concave angle, creating a very thin but sharp edge.

Hone To sharpen on a fine-grained whetstone or on a steel.

Iron A heavy metal used as the base in steel alloys; it is malleable when hot.

Mineral oil A clear, mineral-based oil that may be used for lubrication of sharpening stones.

Molybdenum A hard, silvery-white metallic element used to strengthen and harden steel alloys.

NSF International (NSF) An independent, not-for-profit organization that offers programs and services to support the work of regulatory officials around the country, including standards development, product testing, and certification, as well as on-site audits and inspections.

Paring knife A small knife with a blade ranging in length from 2 to 4 inches long and is used primarily for trimming and peeling vegetables.

Partial tang An extension of a knife's blade that extends partway into the handle.

Rat-tail tang An extension of the blade into the handle that is quite narrow in relation to the width of the handle.

Rivets The pieces used to attach the handle to the blade of a knife.

Rockwell scale A scale used to measure the hardness of metals.

Shaft (of a steel) The part of a steel used to hone knives.

Shank *See* Bolster.

Sharpening stone A stone used to sharpen the edge of a dull knife.

Slicer, Slicing knife A long knife with a relatively narrow blade used principally for carving and slicing larger cuts of cooked, roasted, or smoked items.

Sintering Fusing together different parts of a knife from different metals.

Spine The top of a knife blade.

Stamped To cut a shape from a sheet of metal.

Stainless steel Carbon steel with chromium added to inhibit rust and discoloration.

Steel (1) A tool used to maintain knife blades. It is usually made of steel but may be ceramic, glass, or diamond-impregnated metal. Sometimes referred to as a sharpening or honing steel. (2) An alloy of iron with carbon (carbon steel) and perhaps several other metals, including nickel, chromium, and molybdenum, to increase the hardness and/or resilience of the iron.

Steeling To realign, straighten and/or maintain the edge of a knife.

Stone *See* Sharpening stone.

Stone Age The first known period of human culture, characterized by the use of stone tools.

Tang The section of the knife blade that extends into the handle.

Taper-ground A knife edge formed from a single sheet of metal that tapers smoothly from the spine of the knife to the cutting edge.

Tempering (temper) The process of heating and cooling metals and metal alloys in order to bring out desired traits such as strength, flexibility, and stain resistance.

Utility knife A smaller, lighter version of the chef's knife; its blade is usually between 5 and 7 inches long.

Whetstone A crude natural stone strapped to a turning wheel that dips into water so the stone doesn't become hot from friction.

Appendix

Selected Sources for Equipment and Supplies

There are several excellent resources on the Internet to compare features and prices for knives. Some catalogs and Web sites sell a variety of knives. This list includes some European manufacturers from countries including France, Germany, and Italy, as well as domestically produced knives and a selection of Asian brands. If you can, visit a good kitchenware store to test the knife you are interested in to make sure it feels balanced and comfortable in your hand.

Ergo-Chef
Ergo Chef, LLC
35 Eagle Road
Danbury, CT 06810
Tel: (203) 796-0880
Fax: (203) 798-6106
www.ergochef.com

Ergonomically designed knives.

Dexter-Russell
44 River Street
Southbridge, MA 01550
Tel: (508) 765-0201
Fax: (508) 764-2897
www.dexter-russell.com

The largest manufacturer of professional cutlery in the United States.

F. Dick
33 Allen Boulevard
Farmingdale, NY 11735
Tel: (800) 554-3425
Fax: (631) 454-6184
www.fdick.com

German manufacturer of high-quality products since 1778 including knifes, tools, and sharpening kits.

Füritechnics
P.O. Box 642308
San Francisco, CA 94164
Fax: (415) 567-9441
www.furitechnics.com

Australian manufacturer of ergonomically designed knives and kitchen tools.

Global
Manufactured by Yoshikin
Niigata, Japan
www.yoshiken.co.jp/w/index.html

Japanese-manufactured knives, one piece, molybdenum/vanadium stainless steel design.

Misono
Seki, Japan
www.misono-knives.com

The knives produced from this 750-year-old manufacturer are known for their design, quality, and lasting sharpness.

Glestain
Manufactured by Honma Science
Limited
Niigata, Japan
www.glestain-knives.com

Designs and produces the unique Glestain brand knives using advanced, computerized techniques. Glestain's signature Acuto steel is one of the finest stain-resistant knife steels available.

Frost
Mora of Sweden
5475 West Inscription Canyon Drive
Prescott, AZ 86305
Tel: (928) 442-0140
Fax: (928) 442-0342
www.scandia-international.com

J. A. Henckels
Zwilling J. A. Henckels USA
171 Saw Mill River Road
Hawthorne, NY 10532
Tel: (800) 777-4308
Fax: (914) 747-1850
www.jahenckels.com

German-based manufacturer of premium knifes and kitchen tools.

Kershaw Knives (Shun)
Manufactured by KAI USA
18600 SW Teton Avenue
Tualatin, OR 97062
Tel: (503) 682-1966
Fax: (503) 682-7168
www.kershawknives.com

The Shun knife has an edge of only 16 degrees, compared to the average knife at 22, and so stays much sharper than other knives.

Kikuichi
P.O. Box 374
Carlstadt, NJ 07072
Tel: (201) 530-0087
Fax: (201) 530-0097
www.kikuichi.net

Originally a manufacturer of Samurai swords, this Japanese company has been producing superior Western-style chef's knives for the past 100 years.

LamsonSharp
Manufactured by Lamson & Goodnow
15 Greenfield Street
Greenfield, MA 01301
Tel: (800) 872-6564
Fax: (413) 774-7776
www.lamsonsharp.com

American-made cutlery and kitchen tools made from hardened and tempered high-carbon stainless steel.

MAC Knife, Inc.
9624 Kiefer Blvd. #1
Sacramento, CA 95827
Tel: (888) 622-5643
Fax: (916) 854-9974
www.macknife.com

MAC Knives are stamped, not forged. Blades are thin, lightweight, and precise.

Messermeister U.S.
418 Bryant Circle, Suite A
Ojai, CA 93023
Tel: (800) 426-5134
Fax: (805) 640-0051
www.messermeister.com

German-made cutlery forged from high-carbon molybdenum/vanadium steel.

Mundial, Inc.
19 Walpole Park South
Walpole, MA 02081
Tel: (508) 668-7400 or (800) 487-2224
Fax: (508) 668-7470
www.mundialusa.com

Brazilian-manufactured professional quality cutlery.

Nenox USA, Inc.
252 Bogert Road, Suite D
River Edge, NJ 07661
Tel: (201) 489-8204
Fax: (201) 489-8204
www.nenoxusa.com

Japanese-manufactured knives in both the Japanese and Western styles.

Sabatier

Bellevue 63300
Thiers, France
Tel: +33 04 73 80 11 03
www.sabatier.com

Classic French chef's knives forged from Z50C13 steel. Manufactured in France for over 150 years.

Kyocera

17862 Fitch
Irvine, CA 92614
Tel: (800) 537-0294
Fax: (949) 930-0910
http://kyoceraadvancedceramics.com/

Ceramic blades that offer superior edge, retention, and sharpness.

Wusthof-Trident

333 South Highland Avenue
Briarcliff Manor, New York 10510
Tel: (914) 923-6000
Fax: (914) 923-6514
www.wusthof.com

Precision knives forged from high-carbon steel.

Warren Kitchen & Cutlery Brand

6934 Route 9
Rhinebeck, NY 12572
Tel: (845) 876-6208
Fax: (845) 876-0634
www.warrenkitchentools.com

A local favorite of the CIA, Warren manufactures durable, forged high-carbon knives, and also offers a full range of other popular brands.

Victorinox

Schmiedgasse 57 CH-6438
Ibach-Schwyz, Switzerland
Tel: +41 41 81 81 211
Fax: +41 41 81 81 511
www.victorinox.ch

"Perfectly balanced" ergonomic and durable cutlery. Manufactured in Switzerland.

Suppliers

CAD Cutlery

14100 Barbara Circle
Cooksville, MD 21723
Tel: (877) 704-4481
www.cadcutlery.com

Distributors of Forschners, Dexter Russell

Korin

57 Warren Street
New York, NY 10007
Tel: (800) 626-2172 or (212) 587-7021
Fax: (212) 587-7027
www.korin.com
Distributor of Japanese- and Western-style chef's knives as well as kitchen tools and utensils.

Kitchen Knives and Cutlery

P.O. Box 600
5111 Berwyn Road, Suite 110
College Park, MD 20740
Tel: (800) 338-6799
www.knifecenter.com

Distributors of Wusthof, Victorinox, KAI, Henckels, etc.

Knives for Chefs

9325 Vervain Street
San Diego, CA 92129
Tel: (858) 335-6396
www.knivesforchefs.com

Distributors of Messermeister knives and various kitchen tools.

Yamasho, Inc.

750 Touhy Avenue
Elk Grove Village, IL 60007
Tel: (847) 981-9342
Fax: (847) 981-9347
www.yamashoinc.com/index.htm

Supplier for the high-grade Suisin knives, manufactured in Sakai, Japan.

Further Reading and Reference Resources

Chemistry of Cooking

Charley, Helen, and Connie M. Weaver. *Foods: A Scientific Approach,* 3rd ed. Upper Saddle River, NJ: Prentice-Hall, 1997.

Corriher, Shirley. *CookWise: The Secrets of Cooking Revealed.* New York: Morrow/Avon, 1997.

Griswold, Campbell Penfield. *The Experimental Study of Food,* 2nd ed. Boston: Houghton Mifflin, 1979.

McGee, Harold. *The Curious Cook.* New York: Hungry Minds, 1992.

McGee, Harold. *On Food and Cooking: The Science and Lore of the Kitchen.* New York: Scribner, 2004.

Dictionaries and Encyclopedias

Bickel, Walter. *Herings Dictionary of Classical and Modern Cookery.* New York: French and European Publications, 1981.

Cost, Bruce. *Asian Ingredients: A Guide to the Foodstuffs of China, Japan, Korea, Thailand, and Vietnam.* New York: HarperCollins, 2000.

Coyle, Patrick L. *The World Encyclopedia of Food.* New York: Facts on File, 1982.

Davidson, Alan. *The Oxford Companion to Food.* New York: Oxford University Press, 1999.

Del Conte, Anna. *Gastronomy of Italy.* Upper Saddle River, NJ: Prentice-Hall, 1988.

Dowell, Philip and Adrian Bailey. *The Cook's Ingredients.* Pleasantville, NY: Reader's Digest Association, 1990.

Herbst, Sharon. *Food Lover's Companion,* 4th ed. Hauppage, NY: Barron's, 2001.

Jacobs, Jay. *Gastronomy.* New York: Newsweek Books, 1975.

Knight, John B. and Charles A. Salter, eds. *Knight's Foodservice Dictionary.* New York: John Wiley & Sons, 1987.

Lang, Jenifer Harvey, ed. *Larousse Gastronomique.* New York: Crown, 1988.

Maree, Aaron. *Patisserie: An Encyclopedia of Cakes, Pastries, Cookies, Biscuits, Chocolate, Confectionery and Desserts.* New York: HarperCollins, 1994.

Mariani, John F. *The Encyclopedia of American Food and Drink.* New York: Lebhar-Friedman, 1999.

Passmore, Jacki. *The Encyclopedia of Asian Food and Cooking.* New York: Hearst, 1991.

Raymond Oliver. *Gastronomy of France.* Translated by Claud Durrell. New York: Wine & Food Society with World Publishing, 1967.

Riely, Elizabeth. *The Chef's Companion: A Concise Dictionary of Culinary Terms,* 2nd ed. New York: John Wiley & Sons, 1996.

Rubash, Joyce. *The Master Dictionary of Food and Wine,* 2nd ed. New York: John Wiley & Sons, 1996.

Simon, André Louis. *A Concise Encyclopedia of Gastronomy.* New York: Overlook, 1983.

Von Welanetz, Diana, and Paul von Welanetz. *The Von Welanetz Guide to Ethnic Ingredients.* New York: Warner, 1987.

Equipment and Mise en Place

Aronson, Emily, and Florence Fabricant, and Burt Wolf. *The New Cook's Catalogue: The Definitive Guide to Cooking Equipment.* New York: Knopf, 2000.

The Culinary Institute of America. *The Professional Chef's Knife Kit,* 2nd ed. New York: John Wiley & Sons, 1999.

Schmidt, Arno. *The Chef's Book of Formulas, Yields and Sizes,* 3rd ed. Hoboken, NJ: John Wiley & Sons, 2003.

Scriven, Carl, and James Stevens. *Food Equipment Facts: A Handbook for the Foodservice Industry,* 2nd ed. New York: John Wiley & Sons, 1989.

Williams, Chuck. *The Williams-Sonoma Cookbook and Guide to Kitchenware.* New York: Random House, 1986.

General and Classical Cookery

Bennion, Marion. *Introductory Foods*, 11th ed. Upper Saddle River, NJ: Prentice-Hall, 1999.

Bocuse, Paul. *Paul Bocuse's French Cooking*. Translated by Colette Rossant. New York: Pantheon, 1987.

Brillat-Savarin, Jean-Anthelme. *The Physiology of Taste, or Meditations on Transcendental Gastronomy*. Washington, D.C.: Counterpoint, 2000.

Dornenberg, Andrew, and Karen Page. *Culinary Artistry*. New York: John Wiley & Sons, 1991.

Escoffier, Auguste. *Escoffier Cook Book*. New York: Crown, 1941.

Escoffier, Auguste. *Guide Culinaire: The Complete Guide to the Art of Modern Cooking*. Translated by H. L. Cracknell and R. J. Kaufmann. New York: John Wiley & Sons, 1979.

Escoffier, Auguste. *The Complete Guide to the Art of Modern Cookery*. New York: John Wiley & Sons, 1995.

Fuller, John, and Edward Renold and David Faskett. *The Chef's Compendium of Professional Recipes*, 3rd ed. London: Butterworth-Heinemann, 1992.

Gielisse, Victor. *Cuisine Actuelle*. Boulder, CO: Taylor Publications, 1992.

Metz, Ferdinand E. and the U.S. Team. *Culinary Olympics Cookbook: U.S. Team Recipes from the International Culinary Olympics*. Edited by Steve M. Weiss. Silver Spring, MD: Cahners, 1983.

Millau, Christian. *Dining in France*. New York: Stewart, Tabori & Chang, 1986.

Pauli, Eugene. *Classical Cooking the Modern Way*, 3rd ed. New York: John Wiley & Sons, 1999.

Pépin, Jacques. *La Technique*. New York: Simon & Schuster, 1989.

Peterson, James. *Essentials of Cooking*. New York: Artisan, 2000.

Point, Ferdinand. *Ma Gastronomie*. Translated by Frank Kulla and Patricia S. Kulla. Chicago: Lyceum, 1974.

Saulnier, Louis. *Le Répertoire de la Cuisine*. Hauppage, NY: Barron's, 1977.

The Culinary Institute of America. *The Professional Chef*, 8th ed. Hoboken, NJ: John Wiley & Sons, 2006.

The Food and Beverage Institute. Mary D. Donovan, ed. *Cooking Essentials for the New Professional Chef*. New York: John Wiley & Sons, 1997.

Wolfe, Kenneth C. *Cooking for the Professional Chef*. Clifton Park, NY: Delmar, 1982.

Baking and Pastry

Amendola, Joseph. *The Baker's Manual,* 4th ed. New York: John Wiley & Sons, 1993.

Beranbaum, Rose Levy. *The Pie and Pastry Bible*. New York: Simon and Schuster, 1998.

France, Wilfred J. *The New International Confectioner,* 5th ed. New York: Van Nostrand Reihnold, 1981.

Malgieri, Nick. *Nick Malgieri's Perfect Pastry*. New York: Hungry Minds, 1998.

Sultan, William J. *Practical Baking*. New York: John Wiley & Sons, 1996.

Business and Management

Bell, Donald. *Food and Beverage Cost Control*. Berkeley, CA: McCutchen, 1984.

Blocker, Linda, Julie Hill, and The Culinary Institute of America. *Culinary Math*. New York: John Wiley & Sons, 2002.

Crawford, Hattie and Milton McDowell. *Math Workbook for Foodservice and Lodging*. New York: John Wiley & Sons, 1988.

Dornenburg, Andrew, and Karen Page. *Becoming a Chef: With Recipes and Reflections from America's Leading Chefs*. New York: John Wiley & Sons, 1995.

Haines, Robert G. *Math Principles for Food Service Occupations,* 3rd ed. Clifton Park, NY: Delmar, 1995.

Ruhlman, Michael. *The Making of a Chef: Mastering the Heat at the CIA*. New York: Henry Holt, 1997.

Spears, Marion. *Foodservice Organizations,* 4th ed. Upper Saddle River, NJ: Prentice-Hall, 1999.

Trotter, Charlie. *Lessons in Excellence from Charlie Trotter*. Berkeley, CA: Ten Speed Press, 1999.

Whitman, Joan and Dolores Simon. *Recipes into Type: A Handbook for Cookbook Writers and Editors*. New York: Harper-Collins, 1993.

Periodicals and Journals

American Brewer (professional interest, American beers, pubs, and brew houses)

Appellation (wine, with food and travel)

Art Culinaire (professional interest, hard cover, food)

The Art of Eating (general interest, food, travel, photography)

Beverage World (professional interest, all beverages)

Bon Appétit (general interest, food, cooking, wine, travel, entertainment)

Caterer and Hotelkeeper (professional interest from the UK, food reviews from around the world, hotels, food industry)

Chef (professional interest, industry news, food, cooking)

Chocolate News (professional interest, retail information, recipes)

Chocolatier (general interest, chocolate and chocolate recipes, travel)

Cooking for Profit (professional interest, food service equipment, cooking)

Cook's Illustrated (general interest, food, recipes, cooking)

Cooking Light (general interest, healthy food, recipes, cooking)

Culinary Trends (professional interest, cooking travel)

Decanter (professional interest, world wines)

Food and Wine (general interest, food, recipes, wine, cooking, entertaining)

Food Arts (professional interest, restaurant news, trends, foods, recipes)

Food for Thought (professional interest, food, agriculture, nutrition)

Food Management (professional interest, schools, colleges, healthcare, corporate)

Fresh Cup (professional interest, specialty beverages)

Gastronomica (professional interest, food, culture, writing)

Gourmet (general interest, food, recipes, entertainment, cooking)

Herb Companion (general interest, herbs, recipes)

Hospitality (professional interest, hotel and catering industry)

Hospitality Design (professional interest, restaurant and hotel décor and design)

Hotel and Motel Management (professional interest, new, analysis, trends)

Hotels (professional interest, news, analysis, trends, management)

Meat and Poultry (professional interest, meats, poultry, retail, processing)

Modern Baking (professional interest, new, analysis, trends for wholesale and retail)

Nation's Restaurant News (professional interest, news, business, analysis, trends)

Nutrition Action Healthletter (professional interest, nutrition news, analysis, trends)

Prepared Foods (professional interest, news, analysis, trends and technologies for marketers and formulators)

Restaurant Business (professional interest, entrepreneurs, news, analysis, trends)

Restaurant Hospitality (professional interest, news, analysis, trends)

Restaurant and Institutions (professional interest, news, analysis, trends)

Saveur (general interest, writing, food, cuisine, recipes)

Wine and Spirits (professional interest, wine, spirits, travel)

Wine Spectator (general interest, wine, reviews, ratings)

Wines and Vines (professional interest, news and trends in grape production and wine industry)

Sanitation and Safety

Applied Foodservice Sanitation Textbook. Educational Foundation of the National Restaurant Association, 4th ed. New York: John Wiley & Sons, 1992.

Loken, Joan K. *The HACCP Food Safety Manual.* New York: John Wiley & Sons, 1995.

McSwane, David, and Nancy R. Rue and Richard Linton. *Essentials of Food Safety and Sanitation,* 4th ed. Upper Saddle River, NJ: Prentice-Hall, 2004.

Culinary Associations

American Culinary Federation (ACF)
180 Center Place Way
St. Augustine, FL 32095
Tel: (904) 824-4468 or (800) 624-9458
Fax: (904) 825-4758
www.acfchefs.org

American Institute of Wine and Food (AIWF)
213-37 39th Avenue, Box 216
Bayside, NY 11361
Tel: (800) 274-2493
Fax: (718) 522-0204
www.aiwf.org

Chefs Collaborative
89 South Street, Lower Level
Boston, MA 02111
Tel: (617) 236-5200
Fax: (617) 236-5200
www.chefscollaborative.org

Chefs de Cuisine Association of America
155 East 55th Street, Suite 302B
New York, NY 10022
Tel: (212) 832-4939

International Association of Culinary Professionals (IACP)
304 West Liberty, Suite 201
Louisville, KY 40202
Tel: (502) 581-9786 or (800) 928-4227
Fax: (502) 589-3602
www.iacp.com

International Council on Hotel/Restaurant and Institutional Education (CHRIE)
2810 North Parham, Suite 230
Richmond, VA 23294
Tel: (804) 346-4800
Fax: (804) 346-5009
www.chrie.org

International Les Dames d'Escoffier (LDEI), DC Chapter
P.O. Box 1617
Washington, DC 20013
Tel: (202) 973-2168
www.lesdamesdc.org

The James Beard Foundation
167 West 12th Street
New York, NY 10011
Tel: (212) 675-4984 or (800) 36-BEARD
Fax: (212) 645-1438
www.jamesbeard.org

National Restaurant Association (NRA)
1200 17th Street, NW
Washington, DC 20036
Tel: (202) 331-5900
www.restaurant.org

Oldways Preservation and Exchange Trust
25 First Street
Cambridge, MA 01241
Tel: (617) 621-1230

Roundtable for Women in Foodservice
3022 West Eastwood
Chicago, IL 60625
Tel: (800) 898-2849

Share Our Strength (SOS)
1511 K Street, NW, Suite 94
Washington, DC 20005
Tel: (202) 393-2925

Women Chefs and Restaurateurs (WCR)
455 South Fourth Street, Suite 650
Louisville, KY 40202
Tel: (502) 581-0300 or (877) 927-7787
Fax: (502) 589-3602
www.womenchefs.org

Knives and Tools Checklist

Essential Knives and Tools

Boning knife (5-inch)

Carving fork

Chef's knife (10-inch)

Cutting board

Gram/ounce scale

Knife guards and knife carrier

Paring knife (3H-inch)

Pastry bag and tips

Pastry brush

Sharpening steel

Sharpening stone

Slicing knife (10-inch)

Tomato knife (5H-inch)

Utility knife (4-inch)

Optional Knives and Tools

Bread knife (8-inch)

Cheese knife

Cleaver for bones

Heavy chef's knife (8-inch)

Scimitar

Slicing knife (9-inch)

Specialty Knives and Tools

Apple corer

Aspic cutters

Bird's beak/tourné knife

Channel knife

Cheese knife

Flexible filleting knife (fish)

Ice carving tools

Knife block

Olive/cherry pitter

Rigid boning knife (meats)

Sandwich spreader/knife

Sharpening stone

Tweezers and forceps

Zester

Bakeshop Knives and Tools

Bread knife (8-inch)

Biscuit cutters

Cake icing spatulas (palette knife)

Dough scraper (bench scraper)

Gram/ounce scale

Measuring spoons, cups, pitchers

Offset spatula

Paring knife (3H-inch)

Pastry bag and tips

Pastry blender

Pastry brush

Pastry cloth

Portioning scoops

Rolling pin and cover

Slicing knife (9-inch)

Common Yields from Selected Foods

INGREDIENT	DETAILS	VOLUME	WEIGHT (U.S.)	WEIGHT (METRIC)
Apple	1 medium	1 cup sliced	4.2 ounces	119 grams
Asparagus	1 bunch	2 cups	9.5 ounces	269 grams
Bacon	1 cooked strip, crumbled	2 tablespoons	.75 ounce	21 grams
Baking powder		1 teaspoon	.15 ounce	4 grams
Baking soda		1 teaspoon	.18 ounce	5 grams
Beans	Black, garbanzo (chickpeas), lima, pinto	1 cup dried	6.5 ounces	184 grams
	Cannellini	1 cup dried	7.25 ounces	206 grams
Bell pepper	1 medium	1⅓ cups diced	7 ounces	198 grams
Bread crumbs	5 slices of bread	1 cup crumbs	3.5 ounces	100 grams
Broccoli	1 head	3½ cups florets (approx.)	8.75 ounces	248 grams
Butter	1 stick	8 tablespoons	4 ounces	113 grams
	1 pound whole	1¾ cups clarified	12 ounces	355 grams
Cabbage		1 cup shredded	3.3 ounces	94 grams
	1 small head	8 cups shredded (approx.)	26 ounces	737 grams
Capers		1 tablespoon	.25 ounce	7 grams
Carrot		1 cup diced	5 ounces	142 grams
	1 medium	½ cup diced (approx.)	3.3 ounces	94 grams
Cauliflower		1 cup florets	4.7 ounces	133 grams
	1 head	3¾ cups florets (approx.)	18 ounces	510 grams
Celeriac (celery root)		1 cup diced	3 ounces	85 grams
	1 medium	3½ cups diced (approx.)	12 ounces	340 grams
Celery (Pascal)		1 cup diced	4 ounces	113 grams
	1 stalk	½ cup diced (approx.)	2 ounces	57 grams
Cheese				
	Hard (e.g., Parmesan)	1 cup grated	3.75 ounces	106 grams
	Medium (e.g., Cheddar)	1 cup shredded	3 ounces	85 grams
	Soft (e.g., fresh goat or blue)	1 cup crumbled	4.75 ounces	135 grams
Chocolate chips		1 cup	5.5 ounces	156 grams
Coconut (fresh)		1 cup shredded	2.75 ounces	78 grams

INGREDIENT	DETAILS	VOLUME	WEIGHT (U.S.)	WEIGHT (METRIC)
Coconut (dried)		1 cup shredded	2.4 ounces	68 grams
Corn		1 cup kernels	5.75 ounces	163 grams
	1 ear	½ cup kernels (approx.)	2.75 ounces	78 grams
Cornstarch		1 tablespoon	.3 ounce	8. 5 grams
Eggplant		1 cup diced	3 ounces	85 grams
	1 medium globe	3 cups diced (approx.)	9 ounces	255 grams
Garlic		1 tablespoon minced	.25 ounce	7 grams
	1 clove	1 teaspoon minced (approx.)	.125 ounce	3 grams
Ginger		1 teaspoon grated	.15 ounce	4 grams
Green onion		1 cup sliced	2 ounces	57 grams
	1 medium	¼ cup sliced (approx.)	.5 ounce	14 grams
Ham		1 cup minced	4 ounces	113 grams
Herbs (dried)		1 tablespoon	.08 ounce	225 milligrams
Herbs (fresh)		1 tablespoon minced	.115 ounce	3 grams
Honey		1 tablespoon	.75 ounce	21 grams
Jalapeño		1 teaspoon minced	.10 ounce	3 grams
	1 medium	2 tablespoons minced (approx.)	.5 ounce	14 grams
Jícama		1 cup diced	4.5 ounces	128 grams
Juniper berries		1 tablespoon	.176 ounce	5 grams
Kale		1 cup chopped	2.5 ounces	71 grams
Leek		1 cup sliced	4 ounces	113 grams
	1 leek, white and green parts	1¼ cups sliced (approx.)	6 ounces	170 grams
Lemon	1 medium, juiced	3 tablespoons	1.5 ounces	43 grams
	1 medium, zested	2 teaspoons	.10 ounce	3 grams
Lentils		1 cup dry	6 ounces	170 grams
Lime	1 medium, juiced	3 tablespoons	1.5 ounces	43 grams
	1 medium, zested	2 teaspoons	.10 ounce	3 grams
Mushroom		1 cup sliced (approx.)	2 ounces	57 grams
	1 large white mushroom	¼ cup sliced (approx.)	.5 ounce	14 grams
Mustard (prepared)		1 tablespoon	.5 ounce	14 grams
Nuts		1 cup chopped	4 ounces	113 grams

INGREDIENT	DETAILS	VOLUME	WEIGHT (U.S.)	WEIGHT (METRIC)
Onion		1 cup diced	4 ounces	113 grams
	1 medium	1¾ cups diced (approx.)	7 ounces	198 grams
Orange	1 medium, juiced	½ cup	4 ounces	113 grams
	1 medium, zested	1 tablespoon	.25 ounce	7 grams
Peas		1 cup	3.5 ounces	100 grams
Pepper (ground)		1 teaspoon	.07 ounce	2 grams
Potato		1 cup diced	5 ounces	142 grams
	1 medium russet	1 cup diced (approx.)	5 ounces	142 grams
	1 medium Yukon gold	¾ cup diced	4 ounces	113 grams
	1 medium red potato	½ cup diced	2 ounces	57 grams
	1 medium sweet potato	1 cup diced	4.5 ounces	128 grams
Radish		1 cup sliced	4 ounces	113 grams
Raisins		1 cup	6 ounces	170 grams
Rice	Converted, long grain	1 cup uncooked	6.5 ounces	184 grams
Saffron threads		1 teaspoon crushed	.025 ounce	71 milligrams
Salad greens	Green leaf lettuce, Boston lettuce	1 cup	2 ounces	57 grams
	Arugula	1 cup	2.5 ounces	71 grams
	Escarole	1 cup chopped	2.5 ounces	71 grams
Salt (table)		1 teaspoon	.25 ounce	7 grams
Seeds (sesame, cumin, fennel, etc.)		1 teaspoon	.20 ounce	6 grams
Shallot		1 teaspoon minced	.125 ounce	3.5 grams
	1 medium	2 tablespoons minced (approx.)	.75 ounce	21 grams
Spices (ground)		1 teaspoon	.07 ounce	2 grams
Spinach		1 cup chopped	2.75 ounces	78 grams
	1 bunch	4 cups chopped (approx.)	10.5 ounces	298 grams
Tomato	1 medium	1 cup chopped	5.75 ounces	163 grams
Turnip		1 cup diced	4.5 ounces	128 grams
Zucchini		1 cup diced	4 ounces	113 grams
	1 medium	2 cups diced	8 ounces	227 grams

Measures and Conversions

Weight Measures Conversions between U.S. and Metric Measurement Systems

U.S.	METRIC*
¼ ounce	8 grams
½ ounce	15 grams
1 ounce	30 grams
4 ounces	115 grams
8 ounces (½ pound)	225 grams
16 ounces (1 pound)	450 grams
32 ounces (2 pounds)	900 grams
40 ounces (2¼ pounds)	1 kilogram

*Metric values have been rounded.

Volume Measures Conversions between U.S. and Metric Measurement Systems

U.S.	METRIC*
1 teaspoon	5 milliliters
1 tablespoon	15 milliliters
1 fluid ounce (2 tablespoons)	30 milliliters
2 fluid ounces (¼ cup)	60 milliliters
8 fluid ounces (1 cup)	240 milliliters
16 fluid ounces (1 pint)	480 milliliters
32 fluid ounces (1 quart)	950 milliliters (.95 liter)
128 fluid ounces (1 gallon)	3.75 liters

*Metric values have been rounded.

Converting Volume Measures

FLUID OUNCES	GALLONS	QUARTS	PINTS	CUPS	TABLESPOONS	TEASPOONS
128 fluid ounces	1 gallon	4 quarts	8 pints	16 cups	256 tablespoons	768 teaspoons
32 fluid ounces	1/4 gallon	1 quart	2 pints	4 cups	64 tablespoons	192 teaspoons
16 fluid ounces	1/8 gallon	1/2 quart	1 pint	2 cups	32 tablespoons	96 teaspoons
8 fluid ounces	NA	1/4 quart	1/2 pint	1 cup	16 tablespoons	48 teaspoons
1 fluid ounce	NA	NA	NA	1/8 cup	2 tablespoons	6 teaspoons

Temperature Conversions

DEGREES FAHRENHEIT (°F)	DEGREES CELSIUS (°C)*
32°	0°
40°	4°
140°	60°
150°	65°
160°	70°
170°	75°
212°	100°
275°	135°
300°	150°
325°	165°
350°	175°
375°	190°
400°	205°
425°	220°
450°	230°
475°	245°
500°	260°

*Celsius temperatures have been rounded.

Weights and Measures Equivalents

pinch	less than ⅛ teaspoon
3 teaspoons	1 tablespoon (½ fluid ounce)
2 tablespoons	⅛ cup (1 fluid ounce)
4 tablespoons	¼ cup (2 fluid ounces)
5⅓ tablespoons	⅓ cup (2⅔ fluid ounces)
8 tablespoons	½ cup (4 fluid ounces)
10⅔ tablespoons	⅔ cup (5⅓ fluid ounces)
12 tablespoons	¾ cup (6 fluid ounces)
14 tablespoons	⅞ cup (7 fluid ounces)
16 tablespoons	1 cup
1 gill	½ cup
1 cup	8 fluid ounces (240 milliliters)
2 cups	1 pint (480 milliliters)
2 pints	1 quart (approximately 1 liter)
4 quarts	1 gallon (3.75 liters)
8 quarts	1 peck (8.8 liters)
4 pecks	1 bushel (35 liters)
1 ounce	28.35 grams (rounded to 30)
16 ounces	1 pound (453.59 grams, rounded to 450)
1 kilogram	2.2 pounds

Information, Hints, and Tips for Calculations

1 gallon = 4 quarts = 8 pints = 16 cups (8 fluid ounces each) = 128 fluid ounces
1 fifth bottle = approximately 1½ pints or exactly 25.6 fluid ounces
1 measuring cup holds 8 fluid ounces (a coffee cup generally holds 6 fluid ounces)
1 egg white = 2 fluid ounces (average)
1 lemon = 1 to 1¼ fluid ounces of juice
1 orange = 3 to 3¼ fluid ounces of juice

To convert ounces and pounds to grams: multiply ounces by 28.35; multiply pounds by 453.59

To convert Fahrenheit to Celsius: $(°F - 32) \times 5/9 = °C$

To round to the next closest whole number, round up if final decimal is 5 or greater; round down if less than 5

Index

Page numbers in *italics* indicate illustrations

Photography Credits

BEN FINK

63, 64, 69, 77, 79, 80, 81, 83, 84, 85, 87, 89, 91, 92, 93, 95, 97, 103, 104, 110, 111, 113, 114, 115, 119, 121, 122, 123, 124, 125, 129, 135

DENNIS GOTTLIEB

iii, 2, 9, 12, 15, 18, 20, 23, 27, 28, 54, 56, 58, 59, 62, 66, 67, 68, 70, 71, 72, 73, 101, 106, 107, 108, 133, 136, 138, 139, 141, 142, 144, 145